5B

PRIMARY MATHEMATICS Standards Edition

TEXTBOOK

W9-AZC-708

mc Marshall Cavendish Education

SM Singapore Math Inc®

Blank

Original edition published under the title Primary Mathematics Textbook 5B
© 1984 Curriculum Planning & Development Division, Ministry of Education, Singapore
Published by Times Media Private Limited

This edition © 2008 Marshall Cavendish International (Singapore) Private Limited
© 2014 Marshall Cavendish Education Pte Ltd
(Formerly known as Marshall Cavendish International (Singapore) Private Limited)

Published by Marshall Cavendish Education
Times Centre, 1 New Industrial Road, Singapore 536196
Customer Service Hotline: (65) 6213 9444
US Office Tel: (1-914) 332 8888 l Fax: (1-914) 332 8882
E-mail: tmesales@mceducation.com
Website: www.mceducation.com

Marshall Cavendish Corporation
99 White Plains Road
Tarrytown, NY 10591
U.S.A.
Tel: (1-914) 332 8888
Fax: (1-914) 332 8882
E-mail: mcc@marshallcavendish.com
Website: www.marshallcavendish.com

Singapore Math Inc®
Distributed by
Singapore Math Inc.®
19535 SW 129th Avenue
Tualatin, OR 97062
U.S.A.
Website: www.singaporemath.com

First published 2008
Reprinted 2009, 2010 (twice), 2011, 2012 (twice), 2014, 2015

Primary Mathematics (Standards Edition) Textbook 5B
ISBN 978-0-7614-6986-5

Printed in Malaysia

Primary Mathematics (Standards Edition) is adapted from Primary Mathematics Textbook 5B (3rd Edition), originally
developed by the Ministry of Education, Singapore. This edition contains new content developed by Marshall Cavendish
International (Singapore) Private Limited, which is not attributable to the Ministry of Education, Singapore.

We would like to acknowledge the Project Team from the Ministry of Education, Singapore, that developed the original
Singapore Edition:
Project Director: Dr Kho Tek Hong
Team Members: Hector Chee Kum Hoong, Liang Hin Hoon, Lim Eng Tann,
              Rosalind Lim Hui Cheng, Ng Hwee Wan, Ng Siew Lee
Curriculum Specialists: Christina Cheong Ngan Peng, Ho Juan Beng

Our thanks to Richard Askey, Emeritus Professor of Mathematics (University of Wisconsin, Madison) and Madge Goldman,
President (Gabriella and Paul Rosenbaum Foundation), for their help and advice in the production of Primary Mathematics
(Standards Edition).

We would also like to recognize the contributions of Jennifer Kempe (Curriculum Advisor, Singapore Math Inc.®) and
Bill Jackson (Math Coach, School No. 2, Paterson, New Jersey) to Primary Mathematics (Standards Edition).

Mathematics Content Standards for California Public Schools reproduced by permission, California Department of Education,
CDE Press, 1430 N Street, Suite 3207, Sacramento, CA 95814.

PREFACE

PRIMARY MATHEMATICS (Standards Edition) is a complete program from the publishers of Singapore's successful *Primary Mathematics* series. Newly adapted to align with the Mathematics Framework for California Public Schools, the program aims to equip students with sound concept development, critical thinking and efficient problem-solving skills.

Mathematical concepts are introduced in the opening pages and taught to mastery through specific learning tasks that allow for immediate assessment and consolidation.

The modeling method enables students to visualize and solve mathematical problems quickly and efficiently.

The Concrete → Pictorial → Abstract approach enables students to encounter math in a meaningful way and translate mathematical skills from the concrete to the abstract.

The **pencil icon** [Exercise 18, pages 18-20] provides quick and easy reference from the Textbook to the relevant Workbook pages. The **direct correlation** of the Workbook to the Textbook facilitates focused review and evaluation.

New mathematical concepts are introduced through a **spiral progression** that builds on concepts already taught and mastered.

Metacognition is employed as a strategy for learners to monitor their thinking processes in problem solving. Speech and thought bubbles provide guidance through the thought processes, making even the most challenging problems accessible to students.

The color patch [ ] is used to invite active student participation and to facilitate lively discussion about the mathematical concepts taught.

Regular **reviews** in the Textbook provide consolidation of concepts learned.

The **glossary** effectively combines pictorial representation with simple mathematical definitions to provide a comprehensive reference guide for students.

---

7 Multiplication by a 2-digit Whole Number

(a) Multiply 2187 by 32.

Estimate:
2187 × 32 ≈ 2000 × 30
= 60,000

The answer 69,984 is close to the estimate 60,000.
The answer is reasonable.

(b) Multiply 21.87 by 32.

Estimate:
21.87 × 32 ≈ 20 × 30
= 600

Remember to place the decimal point correctly.

How would you use (a) to find (b) more quickly!

The answer 699.84 is close to the estimate 600.
The answer is reasonable.

31

∠p, ∠q and ∠r are **angles on a straight line**.
Measure the unknown angles.

∠p = 50°
∠q = [ ]°
∠r = [ ]°
∠p + ∠q + ∠r = [ ]°

AOB is a straight line

The sum of the angles on a straight line is **180°**.

∠x, ∠y and ∠z are **angles at a point**.
Measure the unknown angles.

∠x = 60°
∠y = [ ]°
∠z = [ ]°
∠x + ∠y + ∠z = [ ]°

The 3 marked angles meet at a common point.

The sum of the angles at a point is **360°**.

79

REVIEW 10

1. Find the value of each of the following:
   (a) 16 + 3 × 8 ÷ 4
   (b) 30 + 85 × 2 ÷ (8 + 9)
   (c) (220 ÷ 11) × (28 − 5)
   (d) 12 + (30 − 14) ÷ 4 × 5

2. Find the answer, rounded to the nearest whole number.
   (a) 2.56 × 32
   (b) 45.62 × 0.6
   (c) 56.32 ÷ 3.2

3. $\frac{2}{3}$ of a box of paper clips are red and the rest are green. If there are 120 red paper clips, how many green paper clips are there?

4. Mr. Reed packed $\frac{3}{4}$ kg of cookies equally into 3 bags. Find the weight of each bag of cookies. Give the answer in kilograms.

5. Mr. Lee's monthly salary is $2500. He gives $\frac{1}{5}$ of it to his wife and spends $\frac{3}{4}$ of the remainder. How much money does he spend each month?

6. The lengths of 3 rods are in the ratio 1 : 3 : 4. If the total length is 96 cm, find the length of the longest rod.

7. Carlos has $2.50. Tom has twice as much as Carlos. Ryan has $5 more than Tom. How much do the three boys have altogether?

8. After cutting off a length of 6.32 m from a rope 20 m long, the remainder is divided into 8 equal pieces. What is the length of each piece? Give the answer in meters.

9. What percentage of each figure is shaded?
   (a)
   (b)

10. Express 80% as a decimal.

103

GLOSSARY

Word	Meaning
average	The total value of a set of data, divided by the number or frequency of that data.
coordinates	We can find any point on a graph by naming the **coordinates** of that point. These are ordered pairs of numbers. Example: Point A: (4, 2). The first number, 4, in (4, 2) is the x-coordinate. The second number, 2, is the y-coordinate.
graph	A (coordinate) graph has a horizontal and a vertical number line, called x-axis and y-axis respectively. The two lines intersect at the point (0, 0), called the origin.

174

CONTENTS

7 DECIMALS

1 Tenths, Hundredths and Thousandths

John jumped a distance of 0.83 m in the standing broad jump.

Divide 1 m into 10 equal parts.
Each part is 0.1 m.
8 parts make up 0.8 m.

0.83 m is 0.03 m more than 0.8 m.

1 m

0.8 m

Divide 0.1 m into 10 equal parts.
Each part is 0.01 m.
3 parts make up 0.03 m.

0.1 m

0.03 m

$$0.83 = 0.8 + 0.03$$

0.83 is 8 tenths and 3 hundredths.
0.83 is also 83 hundredths.

$$0.83 = \frac{8}{10} + \frac{3}{100}$$

$$0.83 = \frac{83}{100}$$

1.

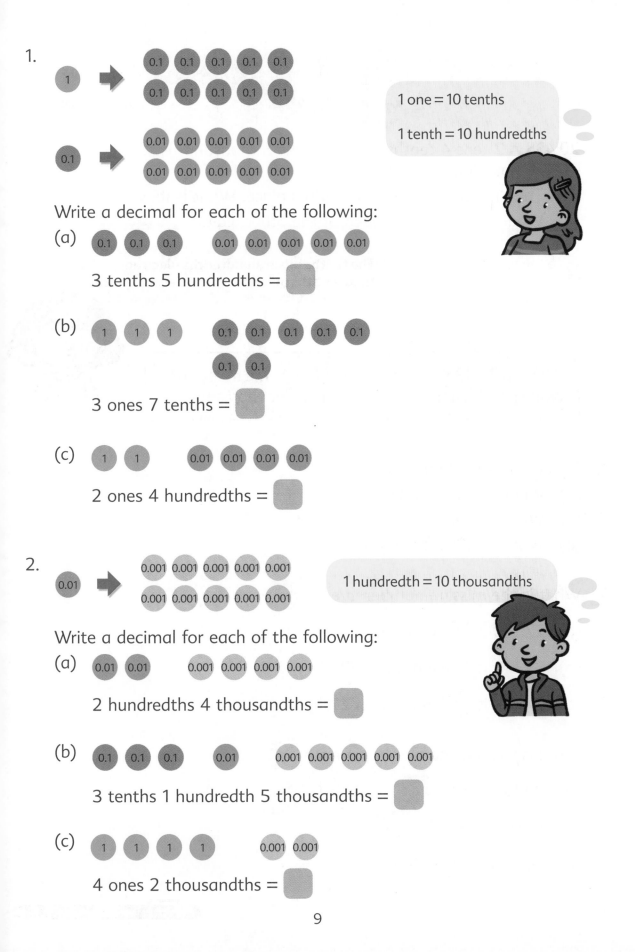

1 one = 10 tenths

1 tenth = 10 hundredths

Write a decimal for each of the following:

(a) 3 tenths 5 hundredths = ☐

(b) 3 ones 7 tenths = ☐

(c) 2 ones 4 hundredths = ☐

2.

1 hundredth = 10 thousandths

Write a decimal for each of the following:

(a) 2 hundredths 4 thousandths = ☐

(b) 3 tenths 1 hundredth 5 thousandths = ☐

(c) 4 ones 2 thousandths = ☐

9

3.

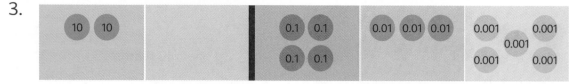

20.435 = 2 tens 4 tenths 3 hundredths 5 thousandths
20.435 has 3 decimal places.

(a) The digit 5 is in the thousandths place. What is its value?

(b) What is the value of each of the other digits?

> The **tenths place, hundredths place** and **thousandths place** are called **decimal places**.

> We read 20.435 as twenty point four three five, or as twenty and four hundred and thirty-five thousandths.

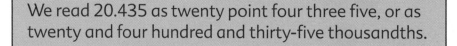

4. (a) What is 0.01 more than 5.62?

(b) What is 0.01 less than 5.62?

(c) What is 0.001 more than 4.536?

(d) What is 0.001 less than 4.536?

5. What is the missing number in each ▢ ?

(a) 27.148 is ▢ more than 27.

(b) 27.148 is ▢ more than 27.1.

(c) 27.148 is ▢ more than 27.14.

6. What is the missing number in each ▢ ?

(a) 30.134 = 30 + ▢ + 0.03 + 0.004

(b) 4.506 = 4 + 0.5 + ▢

(c) 30.023 = ▢ + 0.023

Exercise 1, page 5

7. What number does each letter represent?

(a)

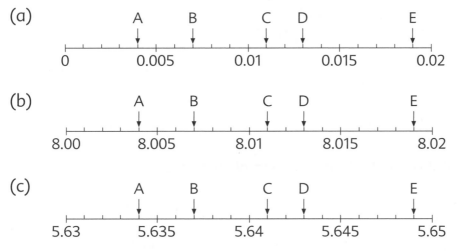

(b)

(c)

8. (a) Which is greater, 42.54 or 42.326?

Tens	Ones	· Tenths	Hundredths	Thousandths
4	2	**5**	4	0
4	2	**3**	2	6

(b) Which is smaller, 63.182 or 63.187?

Tens	Ones	· Tenths	Hundredths	Thousandths
6	3	1	8	**2**
6	3	1	8	**7**

9. Write >, <, or = in each ◯.

(a) 4.6 ◯ 4.58

(b) 26.98 ◯ 27.2

(c) 1.008 ◯ 1.1

(d) 6.328 ◯ 6.325

(e) 12.439 ◯ 12.34

(f) 15.004 ◯ 15.04

10. Arrange the numbers in decreasing order.
    (a) 0.32, 0.302, 0.032, 3.02
    (b) 2.139, 2.628, 2.045, 2.189

11. Arrange the numbers in increasing order.
    (a) 5.8, 0.538, 0.83, 3.58
    (b) 9.047, 9.076, 9.074, 9.067

12. Express 0.052 as a fraction in its simplest form.

$$0.052 = \frac{\overset{13}{\cancel{52}}}{\underset{250}{\cancel{1000}}}$$

$$= \boxed{}$$

0.052 = 52 thousandths

$$= \frac{52}{1000}$$

The simplified form of $\frac{52}{1000}$ is $\frac{13}{250}$.

13. Express each decimal as a fraction in its simplest form.
    (a) 0.5   (b) 0.08
    (c) 0.25   (d) 0.48
    (e) 0.006   (f) 0.024
    (g) 0.345   (h) 0.528

14. Express 2.045 as a fraction in its simplest form.

$$2.045 = 2\frac{45}{1000}$$

$$= \boxed{}$$

15. Express each decimal as a fraction in its simplest form.
    (a) 2.6   (b) 3.2
    (c) 1.25   (d) 6.05
    (e) 3.002   (f) 2.075
    (g) 2.408   (h) 4.125

Exercise 2, page 6

② Approximation

The weight of the watermelon is 2.728 kg.

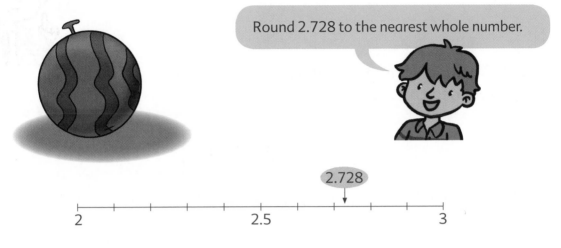

2.728 is more than halfway between 2 and 3. It is rounded to 3.

We write:

$$2.728 \approx 3$$

The weight of the watermelon is **about** 3 kg.

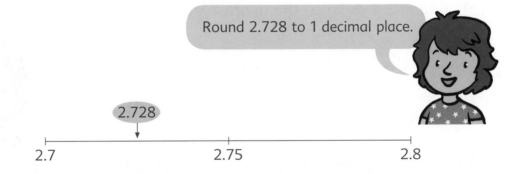

2.728 is less than halfway between 2.7 and 2.8. It is rounded to 2.7.

We write:

$$2.728 \approx 2.7$$

The weight of the watermelon is **about** 2.7 kg.

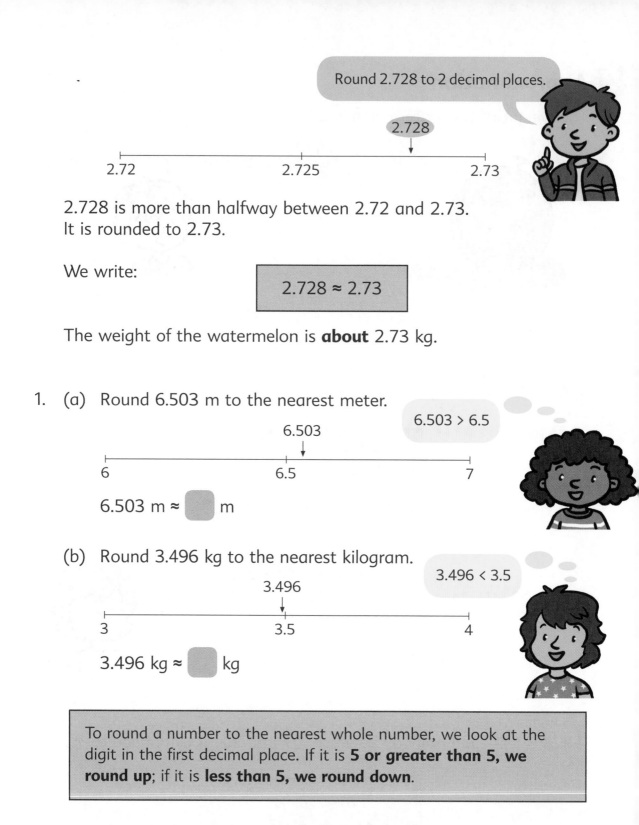

Round 2.728 to 2 decimal places.

2.728

2.72   2.725   2.73

2.728 is more than halfway between 2.72 and 2.73.
It is rounded to 2.73.

We write:

2.728 ≈ 2.73

The weight of the watermelon is **about** 2.73 kg.

1. (a) Round 6.503 m to the nearest meter.

6.503 > 6.5

6.503

6   6.5   7

6.503 m ≈ ⬜ m

(b) Round 3.496 kg to the nearest kilogram.

3.496 < 3.5

3.496

3   3.5   4

3.496 kg ≈ ⬜ kg

To round a number to the nearest whole number, we look at the digit in the first decimal place. If it is **5 or greater than 5, we round up**; if it is **less than 5, we round down**.

2. Round each of the following to the nearest whole number.
   (a) 1.92   (b) 3.18   (c) 18.507   (d) 9.289

3.

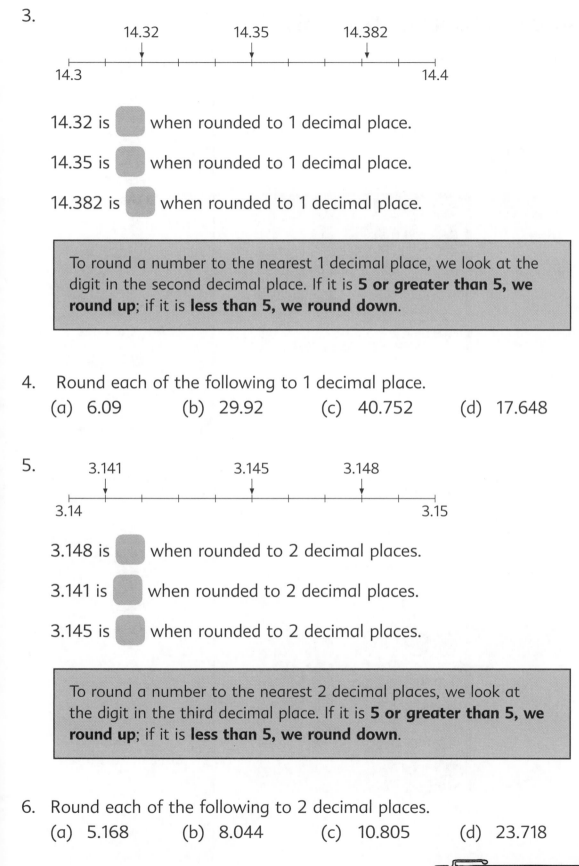

14.32 is [ ] when rounded to 1 decimal place.

14.35 is [ ] when rounded to 1 decimal place.

14.382 is [ ] when rounded to 1 decimal place.

To round a number to the nearest 1 decimal place, we look at the digit in the second decimal place. If it is **5 or greater than 5, we round up**; if it is **less than 5, we round down**.

4. Round each of the following to 1 decimal place.
   (a) 6.09   (b) 29.92   (c) 40.752   (d) 17.648

5.

3.148 is [ ] when rounded to 2 decimal places.

3.141 is [ ] when rounded to 2 decimal places.

3.145 is [ ] when rounded to 2 decimal places.

To round a number to the nearest 2 decimal places, we look at the digit in the third decimal place. If it is **5 or greater than 5, we round up**; if it is **less than 5, we round down**.

6. Round each of the following to 2 decimal places.
   (a) 5.168   (b) 8.044   (c) 10.805   (d) 23.718

Exercise 3, page 7

③ Add and Subtract Decimals

Add 2.63 and 3.84.

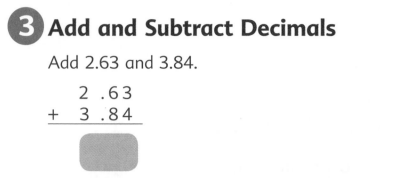

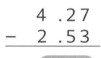

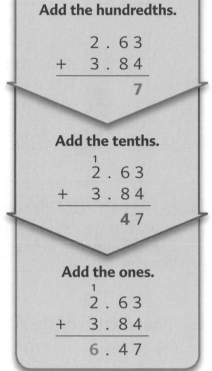

Add the hundredths.

```
  2 . 6 3
+ 3 . 8 4
─────────
        7
```

Add the tenths.

```
    1
  2 . 6 3
+ 3 . 8 4
─────────
      4 7
```

Add the ones.

```
    1
  2 . 6 3
+ 3 . 8 4
─────────
  6 . 4 7
```

Subtract 2.53 from 4.27.

```
  4 . 2 7
− 2 . 5 3
```

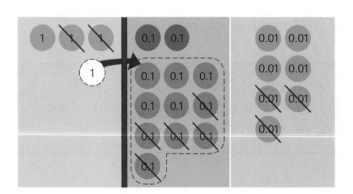

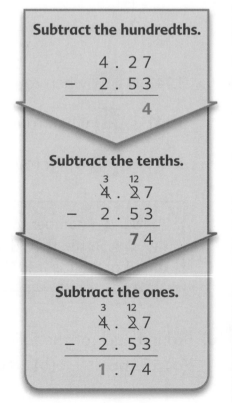

Subtract the hundredths.

```
  4 . 2 7
− 2 . 5 3
─────────
        4
```

Subtract the tenths.

```
    3   12
  4 . 2 7
− 2 . 5 3
─────────
      7 4
```

Subtract the ones.

```
    3   12
  4 . 2 7
− 2 . 5 3
─────────
  1 . 7 4
```

1. What is the answer?
   (a) Add 4 tenths to 4.536.
   (b) Add 3 thousandths to 4.536.
   (c) Subtract 2 hundredths from 4.536.
   (d) Subtract 6 thousandths from 4.536.

2. Find the value of
   (a) 2.465 + 0.2   (b) 3.842 − 0.6
   (c) 1.246 + 0.03   (d) 4.567 − 0.04
   (e) 3.125 + 0.004   (f) 2.043 − 0.002
   (g) 6.1 + 0.006   (h) 5.208 − 0.008

3. What must be added to 0.456 to give the answer 1?

   456 + 544 = 1000
   0.456 + 0.544 = 1

4. Find the missing number.
   (a) 1 − ▢ = 0.46   (b) 1 − ▢ = 0.31   (c) 1 − 0.069 = ▢
   (d) 2 − 1.069 = ▢   (e) 3.42 + ▢ = 5   (f) 12 − 11.111 = ▢

5. Estimate, and then find the value of 1.3 + 2.93.

   1.3 + 2.93 ≈ ▢

   1.3 + 2.93 = ▢

   1.3 + 2.93 ≈ 1 + 3

6. Estimate, and then find the value of 3.2 − 0.38.

   3.2 − 0.38 ≈ ▢

   3.2 − 0.38 = ▢

   3.2 − 0.38 ≈ 3 − 0.4

7. Estimate, and then find the value of
   (a) 2.4 + 3.75   (b) 8.61 + 6.2   (c) 48.7 + 20.68
   (d) 9.82 − 7.93   (e) 10.3 − 5.19   (f) 63.12 − 5.9

17

Exercise 4, page 8

④ Multiply and Divide Decimals by a 1-Digit Whole Number

Multiply 4.53 by 2.

$$
\begin{array}{r}
4.53 \\
\times \quad 2 \\
\hline
\end{array}
$$

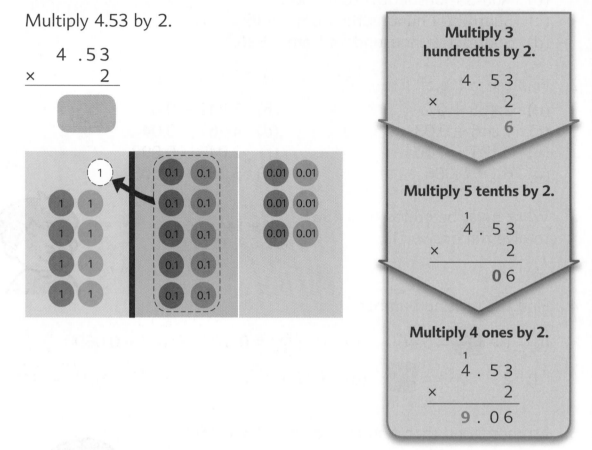

Multiply 3 hundredths by 2.

$$
\begin{array}{r}
4.53 \\
\times \quad 2 \\
\hline
6
\end{array}
$$

Multiply 5 tenths by 2.

$$
\begin{array}{r}
{}^{1} \\
4.53 \\
\times \quad 2 \\
\hline
06
\end{array}
$$

Multiply 4 ones by 2.

$$
\begin{array}{r}
{}^{1} \\
4.53 \\
\times \quad 2 \\
\hline
9.06
\end{array}
$$

Divide 8.1 by 6.

Divide 8 ones by 6.

$$
\begin{array}{r}
1 \\
6{\overline{\smash{)}\,8.1}} \\
6 \\
\hline
2
\end{array}
$$

Divide 21 tenths by 6.

$$
\begin{array}{r}
1.3 \\
6{\overline{\smash{)}\,8.1}} \\
6 \\
\hline
21 \\
18 \\
\hline
3
\end{array}
$$

Divide 30 hundredths by 6.

$$
\begin{array}{r}
1.35 \\
6{\overline{\smash{)}\,8.10}} \\
6 \\
\hline
21 \\
18 \\
\hline
30 \\
30 \\
\hline
0
\end{array}
$$

1. Estimate, and then find the value of 2.08 × 3.

   2.08 × 3 ≈ ◻   2.08 × 3 ≈ 2 × 3

   2.08 × 3 = ◻

2. Estimate, and then find the value of 3.61 ÷ 5.

   3.61 ÷ 5 ≈ ◻   3.61 ÷ 5 ≈ 3.5 ÷ 5

   3.61 ÷ 5 = ◻

3. Estimate, and then find the value of
   (a)   4.82 × 3   (b)   3.63 × 6   (c)   9 × 43.25
   (d)   22.11 ÷ 3   (e)   5.04 ÷ 7   (f)   27.08 ÷ 4

   Exercise 5, page 9

4. (a)   Estimate the value of 21.36 ÷ 9.

   21.36 ÷ 9 ≈ 18 ÷ 9 = 2

   The estimated value is ◻.

   (b)   Find the value of 21.36 ÷ 9 correct to 1 decimal place.

```
      2.37  ≈ 2.4
   9) 2 1.3 6
      1 8
      ─────
        3 3
        2 7
      ─────
          6 6
          6 3
        ─────
            3
```

   Divide to 2 decimal places.
   Then round the answer
   to 1 decimal place.

   The answer is ◻ correct to 1 decimal place.

19

5. (a) Estimate the value of 24.65 ÷ 8.

    24.65 ÷ 8 ≈ 24 ÷ 8 = ⬚

    The estimated value is ⬚.

    (b) Find the value of 24.65 ÷ 8 correct to 2 decimal places.

$$
\begin{array}{r}
3.081 \approx 3.08 \\
8\overline{)24.650} \\
\underline{24} \\
65 \\
\underline{64} \\
10 \\
\underline{8} \\
2
\end{array}
$$

    Divide to 3 decimal places. Then round the answer to 2 decimal places.

    The answer is ⬚ correct to 2 decimal places.

6. Find the value of each of the following correct to 2 decimal places.
    (a) 0.77 ÷ 9   (b) 62.7 ÷ 7   (c) 9.65 ÷ 8
    (d) 41.51 ÷ 6   (e) 27.69 ÷ 4   (f) 20.93 ÷ 3

    Exercise 6, pages 10 - 11

7. Express $\frac{3}{4}$ as a decimal.

    Method 1:   **Method 2:**

    $\frac{3}{4} \xlongequal{\times 25} \frac{75}{100} = $ ⬚ $\frac{3}{4} = 3 \div 4 = $ ⬚

    ×25

8. Express $\frac{1}{8}$ as a decimal. $\frac{1}{8} = 1 \div 8$

9. Express $3\frac{2}{5}$ as a decimal. $3\frac{2}{5} = 3 + 0.4$

10. Express each fraction as a decimal.

    (a) $2\frac{1}{4}$ (b) $4\frac{3}{8}$ (c) $1\frac{4}{5}$ (d) $6\frac{7}{8}$

20

11. Arrange the numbers in increasing order.

$\frac{5}{8}$,   0.652,   2,   0.6

12. (a) Express $\frac{5}{9}$ as a decimal correct to 1 decimal place.

$\frac{5}{9} = 5 \div 9 \approx 0.6$

OR

$\frac{5}{9} = 5 \div 9 = 0.6$ (correct to 1 decimal place)

The answer is ▢ correct to 1 decimal place.

$$\begin{array}{r} 0.55 \approx 0.6 \\ 9\overline{)\,5.00} \\ \underline{4\ 5} \\ 5\ 0 \\ \underline{4\ 5} \\ 5 \end{array}$$

(b) Express $3\frac{5}{9}$ as a decimal correct to 1 decimal place.

$3\frac{5}{9} \approx 3 + 0.6 = 3.6$

The answer is ▢ correct to 1 decimal place.

13. Express each fraction as a decimal correct to 1 decimal place.

(a) $\frac{3}{4}$ (b) $\frac{4}{7}$ (c) $\frac{4}{9}$ (d) $\frac{5}{6}$

(e) $2\frac{2}{3}$ (f) $4\frac{6}{7}$ (g) $3\frac{1}{6}$ (h) $1\frac{8}{9}$

14. Express $4\frac{2}{3}$ as a decimal correct to 2 decimal places.

$\frac{2}{3} \approx$ ▢

$4\frac{2}{3} \approx$ ▢

OR

$4\frac{2}{3} =$ ▢ (correct to 2 decimal places)

The answer is ▢ correct to 2 decimal places.

$$\begin{array}{r} 0.666 \approx 0.67 \\ 3\overline{)\,2.000} \\ \underline{1\ 8} \\ 2\ 0 \\ \underline{1\ 8} \\ 2\ 0 \\ \underline{1\ 8} \\ 2 \end{array}$$

15. Express each fraction as a decimal correct to 2 decimal places.

(a) $\frac{3}{7}$ (b) $\frac{5}{8}$ (c) $\frac{2}{9}$ (d) $\frac{1}{6}$

(e) $5\frac{7}{9}$ (f) $1\frac{1}{3}$ (g) $4\frac{5}{7}$ (h) $8\frac{3}{8}$

Exercise 7, page 12

1. What is the value of the digit 6 in each of the following?
   (a) 1.658   (b) 6.185   (c) 3.069   (d) 5.746

2. (a) What number is 0.1 less than 5.609?
   (b) What number is 0.01 more than 2.809?
   (c) What number is 0.01 less than 13.520?

3. Express each fraction as a decimal.
   (a) $3\frac{7}{1000}$ (b) $\frac{19}{5}$ (c) $6\frac{1}{4}$ (d) $8\frac{1}{8}$

4. Write >, <, or = in each ◯.
   (a) $\frac{47}{1000}$ ◯ 0.047   (b) 0.205 ◯ $\frac{25}{1000}$

   (c) $3\frac{3}{5}$ ◯ 3.69   (d) $\frac{3}{8}$ ◯ 0.065

   (e) 2.8 ◯ $2\frac{4}{5}$ (f) 1.425 ◯ $1\frac{1}{4}$

   (g) 0.035 ◯ $\frac{35}{1000}$ (h) 0.87 ◯ $\frac{78}{100}$

5. Round each of the following to 2 decimal places.
   (a) 0.119   (b) 7.508   (c) 40.082   (d) 81.143
   (e) 0.725   (f) 3.123   (g) 59.005   (h) 18.607

6. Round each of the following to 2 decimal places.
   (a) 6.265 km   (b) 4.083 kg   (c) 0.189ℓ   (d) 20.245ℓ

7. Express each fraction as a decimal correct to 2 decimal places.
   (a) $\frac{1}{8}$ (b) $\frac{4}{7}$ (c) $2\frac{5}{9}$ (d) $5\frac{2}{3}$

8. Find the value of each of the following correct to 2 decimal places.
   (a) 8.047 + 2.296   (b) 14.37 − 6.084
   (c) 0.86 × 7   (d) 37.52 ÷ 8

⑤ Multiplication by Tens, Hundreds or Thousands

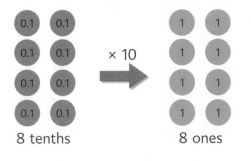 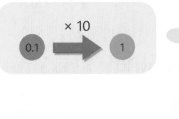 

8 tenths   8 ones

0.8 × 10 = 8

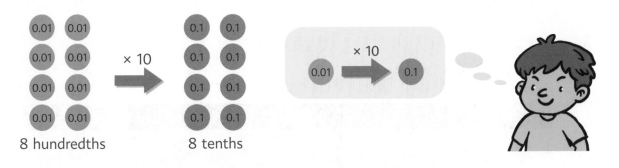

8 hundredths   8 tenths

0.08 × 10 = 0.8

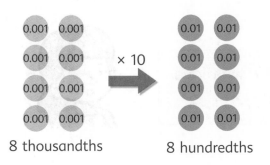 

8 thousandths   8 hundredths

0.008 × 10 = 0.08

1. Multiply.
    (a) 0.6 × 10   (b) 0.8 × 10   (c) 0.9 × 10
    (d) 0.02 × 10   (e) 0.04 × 10   (f) 0.03 × 10
    (g) 0.005 × 10   (h) 0.006 × 10   (i) 0.007 × 10

2. Multiply 3.42 by 10.

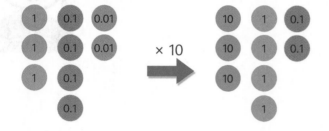

3.42 × 10 = 34.2

3. Multiply 0.035 by 10.

Tens	Ones	•	Tenths	Hundredths	Thousandths
				3	5
			3	5	

0.035 × 10 = 0.35

0.035

> When a decimal is **multiplied by 10**, we move the decimal point **one** place to the **right**.

4. Multiply.
    (a) 0.12 × 10   (b) 0.068 × 10   (c) 0.345 × 10
    (d) 2.05 × 10   (e) 3.21 × 10   (f) 1.439 × 10
    (g) 7.5 × 10   (h) 10.4 × 10   (i) 11.8 × 10

5. Multiply 0.53 by 40.

$$0.53 \times 40 = 2.12 \times 10$$

$$= \boxed{}$$

0.53 × 4 = 2.12

6. Multiply.

(a) 0.006 × 30   (b) 0.08 × 40   (c) 0.9 × 50
(d) 0.32 × 20   (e) 6.81 × 70   (f) 3.248 × 60

Exercise 8, page 13

7. Multiply 0.007 × 100.

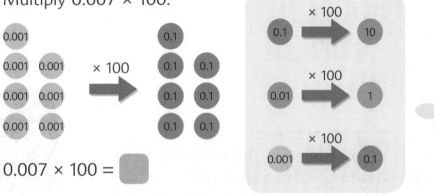

$$0.007 \times 100 = \boxed{}$$

8. Multiply 4.23 by 100.

Hundreds	Tens	Ones	.	Tenths	Hundredths
		4		2	3
4	2	3			

× 100   × 100   × 100

$$4.23 \times 100 = 423$$

4.23

When a decimal is **multiplied by 100**, we move the decimal point **two** places to the **right**.

9. Multiply 0.006 by 1000.

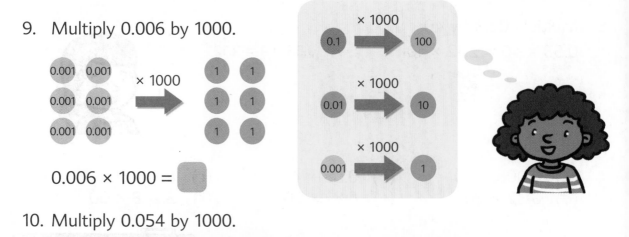

0.006 × 1000 = ☐

10. Multiply 0.054 by 1000.

Tens	Ones	•	Tenths	Hundredths	Thousandths
				5	4
5	4				

×1000   ×1000

0.054 × 1000 = 54

0.054

When a decimal is **multiplied by 1000**, we move the decimal point **three** place to the **right**.

11. Multiply.
   (a) 0.003 × 100   (b) 3.2 × 100   (c) 1.325 × 100
   (d) 0.09 × 1000   (e) 3.62 × 1000   (f) 13.4 × 1000

12. Multiply 4.203 by 200.
   4.203 × 200 = 8.406 × 100   4.203 × 2 = 8.406

   = ☐

13. Multiply 4.203 by 2000.
   4.203 × 2000 = 8.406 × 1000

   = ☐

14. Multiply.
   (a) 0.008 × 300   (b) 0.12 × 600   (c) 1.54 × 400
   (d) 0.03 × 5000   (e) 0.25 × 6000   (f) 5.12 × 4000

26

6 Division by Tens, Hundreds or Thousands

1 1 1	÷ 10 →	0.1 0.1 0.1
3 ones		3 tenths

3 ÷ 10 = 0.3

÷ 10 | 1 → 0.1

0.1 0.1 0.1	÷ 10 →	0.01 0.01 0.01
3 tenths		3 hundredths

0.3 ÷ 10 = 0.03

÷ 10 | 0.1 → 0.01

0.01 0.01 0.01	÷ 10 →	0.001 0.001 0.001
3 hundredths		3 thousandths

0.03 ÷ 10 = 0.003

÷ 10 | 0.01 → 0.001

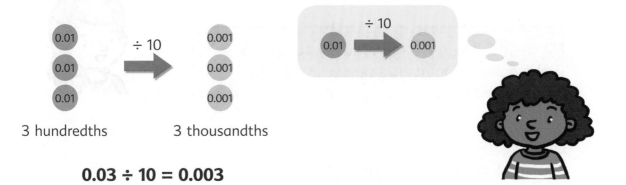

1. Divide.
   (a) 8 ÷ 10   (b) 0.8 ÷ 10   (c) 0.08 ÷ 10
   (d) 2 ÷ 10   (e) 0.2 ÷ 10   (f) 0.02 ÷ 10
   (g) 6 ÷ 10   (h) 0.6 ÷ 10   (i) 0.06 ÷ 10

2. Divide 0.46 by 10.

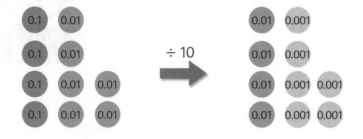

   0.46 ÷ 10 = 0.046

3. Divide 5.3 by 10.

Tens	Ones	•	Tenths	Hundredths	Thousandths
	5		3		
			5	3	

   5.3 ÷ 10 = 0.53

   When a decimal is **divided by 10**, we move the decimal point **one** place to the **left**.

4. Divide.
   (a) 0.23 ÷ 10   (b) 0.45 ÷ 10   (c) 0.12 ÷ 10
   (d) 2.5 ÷ 10   (e) 6.8 ÷ 10   (f) 5.3 ÷ 10
   (g) 12 ÷ 10   (h) 39 ÷ 10   (i) 103 ÷ 10

5. Divide 4.2 by 60.

    $4.2 ÷ 60 = 0.7 ÷ 10$

    $= \boxed{}$

    $4.2 ÷ 6 = 0.7$

6. Divide.

    (a) $8 ÷ 40$ (b) $16 ÷ 80$ (c) $63 ÷ 90$
    (d) $4.8 ÷ 60$ (e) $0.51 ÷ 30$ (f) $3.44 ÷ 80$

Exercise 10, page 16

7. Divide 4 by 100.

    | 1 | 1 | 1 | 1 | ÷ 100 | 0.01 | 0.01 | 0.01 | 0.01 |

    ÷ 100
    10 → 0.1

    ÷ 100
    1 → 0.01

    ÷ 100
    0.1 → 0.001

    $4 ÷ 100 = \boxed{}$

8. Divide 52.8 by 100.

Tens	Ones	.	Tenths	Hundredths	Thousandths
5	2		8		
			5	2	8

÷ 100   ÷ 100   ÷ 100

$52.8 ÷ 100 = 0.528$

52.8

When a decimal is **divided by 100**, we move the decimal point **two** places to the **left**.

29

9. Divide 5 by 1000.

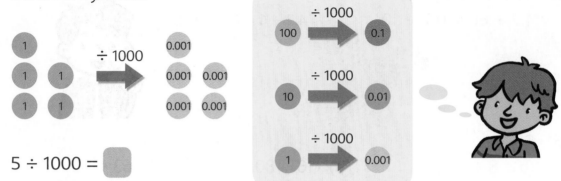

$5 ÷ 1000 = $ ☐

10. Divide 62 by 1000.

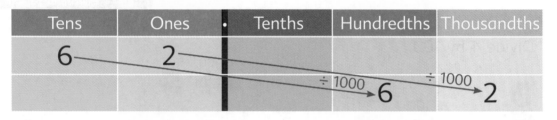

Tens	Ones	•	Tenths	Hundredths	Thousandths
6	2				
				6	2

$62 ÷ 1000 = 0.062$

When a decimal is **divided by 1000**, we move the decimal point **three** places to the **left**.

11. Divide.
    (a) $8 ÷ 100$ (b) $90 ÷ 100$ (c) $1.5 ÷ 100$
    (d) $4 ÷ 1000$ (e) $200 ÷ 1000$ (f) $324 ÷ 1000$

12. Divide 46 by 200.
    $46 ÷ 200 = 23 ÷ 100 = $ ☐

    $46 ÷ 2 = 23$

13. Divide 46 by 2000.
    $46 ÷ 2000 = 23 ÷ 1000 = $ ☐

14. Divide.
    (a) $0.8 ÷ 200$ (b) $1.6 ÷ 400$ (c) $4.8 ÷ 300$
    (d) $12 ÷ 6000$ (e) $65 ÷ 5000$ (f) $714 ÷ 7000$

Exercise 11, pages 17 - 18

7 Multiplication by a 2-Digit Whole Number

(a) Multiply 2187 by 32.

Estimate :
2187 × 32 ≈ 2000 × 30
= 60,000

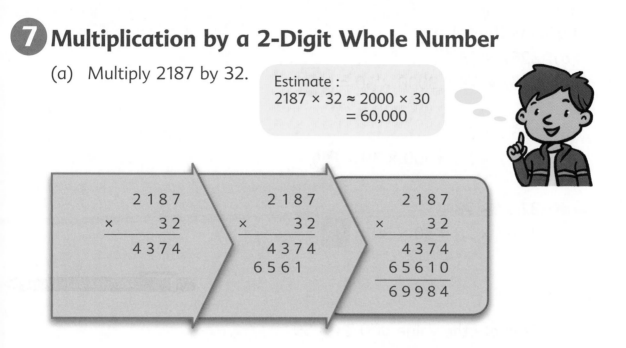

The answer 69,984 is close to the estimate 60,000.
The answer is reasonable.

(b) Multiply 21.87 by 32.

Estimate:
21.87 × 32 ≈ 20 × 30
= 600

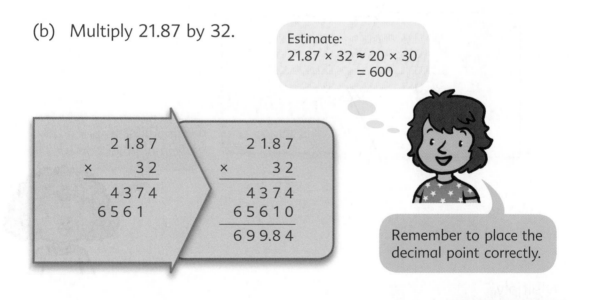

Remember to place the decimal point correctly.

The answer 699.84 is close to the estimate 600.
The answer is reasonable.

How would you use (a) to find (b) more quickly?

1. Estimate the value of
   (a) 3267 × 28
       3267 × 28 ≈ 3000 × 30 =

   (b) 326.7 × 28
       326.7 × 28 ≈ 300 × 30 =

   (c) 32.67 × 28
       32.67 × 28 ≈ 30 × 30 =

Exercise 12, page 19

2. (a) Estimate the value of 0.23 × 59.
       0.23 × 59 ≈ 0.2 × 60 = 12

   (b) Find the value of 0.23 × 59.

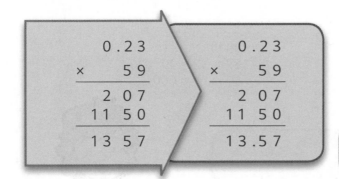

```
    0.23              0.23
  ×   59            ×   59
  ───────           ───────
    2 07              2 07
  11 50             11 50
  ───────           ───────
  13 57             13.57
```

Remember to place the decimal point correctly.

3. Multiply.
   (a) 0.78 × 43   (b) 0.53 × 23   (c) 37 × 4.9
   (d) 23.7 × 26   (e) 40.6 × 45   (f) 18 × 132.4
   (g) 3.58 × 43   (h) 15.09 × 26   (i) 72 × 1.57

Exercise 13, pages 20 - 21

8 Division by a 2-Digit Whole Number

(a) Divide 5928 by 19.

Estimate:
5928 ÷ 19 ≈ 6000 ÷ 20
= 300

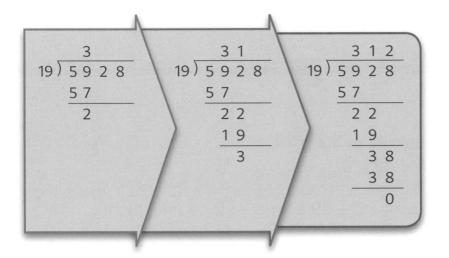

The answer 312 is close to the estimate 300. The answer is reasonable.

(b) Divide 59.28 by 19.

Estimate:
59.28 ÷ 19 ≈ 60 ÷ 20
= 3

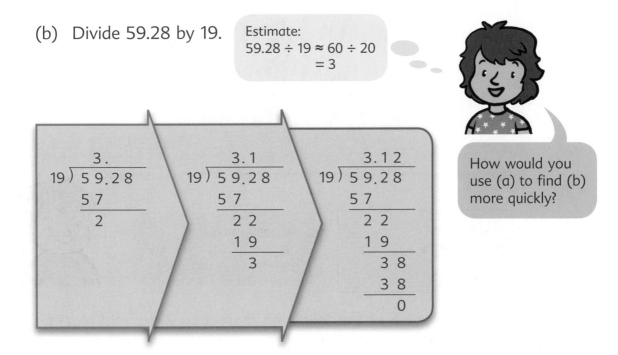

How would you use (a) to find (b) more quickly?

The answer 3.12 is close to the estimate 3. The answer is reasonable.

1. Estimate the value of
   (a) 2877 ÷ 42
       2877 ÷ 42 ≈ 2800 ÷ 40 = ☐

   (b) 287.7 ÷ 42
       287.7 ÷ 42 ≈ 280 ÷ 40 = ☐

   (c) 28.77 ÷ 42
       28.77 ÷ 42 ≈ 28 ÷ 40 = ☐

2. (a) Estimate the value of 5.2 ÷ 29.
       5.2 ÷ 29 ≈ 6 ÷ 30 = 0.2

   (b) Find the value of 5.2 ÷ 29 correct to 2 decimal places.

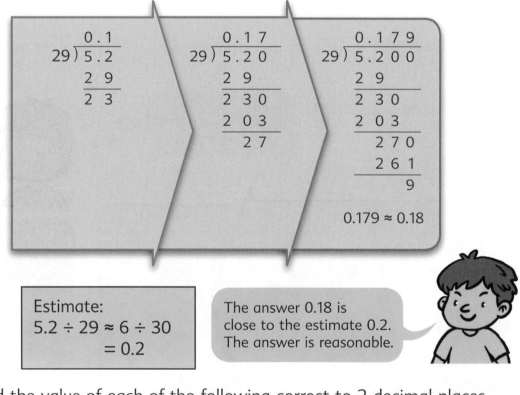

Estimate:
5.2 ÷ 29 ≈ 6 ÷ 30
         = 0.2

The answer 0.18 is close to the estimate 0.2. The answer is reasonable.

3. Find the value of each of the following correct to 2 decimal places.
   (a) 18 ÷ 16   (b) 0.49 ÷ 56   (c) 2.8 ÷ 23
   (d) 62.5 ÷ 31   (e) 15.9 ÷ 29   (f) 9.37 ÷ 32
   (g) 48.6 ÷ 21   (h) 10.28 ÷ 18   (i) 104.8 ÷ 42

Exercise 14, pages 22 - 23

9 Multiplication by a Decimal

$30 \times 0.1 = 30 \times \frac{1}{10}$

$\qquad = \frac{30}{10}$

$\qquad = 3$

$30 \times 0.01 = 30 \times \frac{1}{100}$

$\qquad = \frac{30}{100}$

$\qquad = \frac{3}{10}$

$\qquad = 0.3$

$3 \times 0.1 = 3 \times \frac{1}{10}$

$\qquad = \frac{3}{10}$

$\qquad = 0.3$

$3 \times 0.01 = 3 \times \frac{1}{100}$

$\qquad = \frac{3}{100}$

$\qquad = 0.03$

$0.3 \times 0.1 = \frac{3}{10} \times \frac{1}{10}$

$\qquad = \frac{3}{100}$

$\qquad = 0.03$

$0.3 \times 0.01 = \frac{3}{10} \times \frac{1}{100}$

$\qquad = \frac{3}{1000}$

$\qquad = 0.003$

1. Multiply 4.62 by 0.1.

Tens	Ones	•	Tenths	Hundredths	Thousandths
	4		6	2	
			4	6	2

$4.62 \times 0.1 = 0.462$

When a decimal is **multiplied by 0.1**, we move the decimal point **one** place to the **left**.

2. Multiply 16.3 by 0.01.

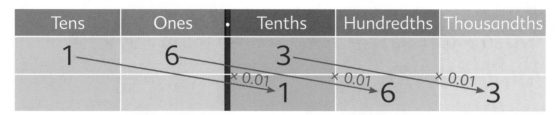

Tens	Ones	•	Tenths	Hundredths	Thousandths
1	6		3		
			1	6	3

$16.3 \times 0.01 = 0.163$

> When a decimal is **multiplied by 0.01**, we move the decimal point **two** places to the **left**.

3. Multiply.
   (a) 0.6×0.1 (b) 0.06×0.1 (c) 5×0.1
   (d) 23×0.1 (e) 3.4×0.1 (f) 0.14×0.1
   (g) 4×0.01 (h) 0.4×0.01 (i) 8×0.01
   (j) 42×0.01 (k) 83.4×0.01 (l) 6.2×0.01

4. Multiply 2.35 by 0.8.

$$2.35 \times 0.8 = 2.35 \times 8 \times 0.1$$
$$= 18.8 \times 0.1$$
$$= 1.88$$

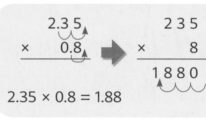

5. Estimate, and then multiply 22.8 by 0.7.

$$22.8 \times 0.7 \approx 20 \times 0.7$$
$$= 14$$

$20 \times 7 = 140$
$20 \times 0.7 = 14$

$22.8 \times 0.7 =$ ⬜

6. Multiply 11.8 by 0.05.

11.8×0.05
$= 11.8 \times 5 \times 0.01$
$= 59 \times 0.01$
$= 0.59$

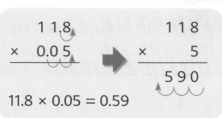

7. Estimate, and then multiply 4.23 by 0.09.

$4.2 \times 0.09 \approx 4 \times 0.09$
$\qquad = 0.36$

> $4 \times 9 = 36$
> $4 \times 0.09 = 0.36$

$4.2 \times 0.09 = \boxed{}$

8. Estimate, and then multiply.
   - (a) 0.3×0.6
   - (b) 4×0.7
   - (c) 0.23×0.5
   - (d) 3.9×0.7
   - (e) 48.2×0.4
   - (f) 9.42×0.3
   - (g) 0.4×0.06
   - (h) 5×0.07
   - (i) 2.9×0.05
   - (j) 3.9×0.04
   - (k) 48.2×0.02
   - (l) 12.7×0.03

> Exercise 15, pages 24 - 25

9. Estimate the value of
   - (a) 3957×49
     $3957 \times 49 \approx 4000 \times 50$
     $= \boxed{}$
   - (b) 395.7×49
     $395.7 \times 49 \approx 400 \times 50$
     $= \boxed{}$
   - (c) 395.7×4.9
     $395.7 \times 4.9 \approx 400 \times 5$
     $= \boxed{}$
   - (d) 395.7×0.49
     $395.7 \times 0.49 \approx 400 \times 0.5$
     $= \boxed{}$
   - (e) 39.57×4.9
     $39.57 \times 4.9 \approx 40 \times 5$
     $= \boxed{}$

> What patterns do you see?

10. (a) Estimate the value of 27.8×0.43.
    $27.8 \times 0.43 \approx 30 \times 0.4$
    $\qquad = 12$

    (b) Multiply 27.8 by 0.43.
    $27.8 \times 0.43 = 27.8 \times 43 \times 0.01$
    $\qquad = 278 \times 0.1 \times 43 \times 0.01$
    $\qquad = 278 \times 43 \times 0.1 \times 0.01$

$$
\begin{array}{r}
2\,7.8 \\
\times \quad 0.4\,3 \\
\end{array}
\qquad
\begin{array}{r}
2\,7\,8 \\
\times \quad 4\,3 \\
\hline
8\,3\,4 \\
1\,1\,1\,2\,0 \\
\hline
1\,1\,9\,5\,4 \\
\end{array}
$$

$2.78 \times 0.43 = 11.954$

11. Multiply.
    - (a) 7.4×4.3
    - (b) 34.12×1.3
    - (c) 9.4×28
    - (d) 72×0.16
    - (e) 8.3×0.21
    - (f) 0.42×65

> Exercise 16, page 26

37

⑩ Division by a Decimal

$30 \div 0.1 = \dfrac{30}{0.1}$

$= \dfrac{30 \times 10}{0.1 \times 10}$

$= \dfrac{300}{1}$

$0.1\overline{)30}$ ➡ $1\overline{)300} = 300$

$30 \div 0.01 = \dfrac{30}{0.01}$

$= \dfrac{30 \times 100}{0.01 \times 100}$

$= \dfrac{3000}{1}$

$0.01\overline{)30}$ ➡ $1\overline{)3000} = 3000$

$30 \div 0.001 = \dfrac{30}{0.001}$

$= \dfrac{30 \times 1000}{0.001 \times 1000}$

$= \dfrac{30,000}{1}$

$0.001\overline{)30}$ ➡ $1\overline{)30,000} = 30,000$

$0.3 \div 0.1 = \dfrac{0.3}{0.1}$

$= \dfrac{0.3 \times 10}{0.1 \times 10}$

$= \dfrac{3}{1}$

$0.1\overline{)0.3}$ ➡ $1\overline{)3} = 3$

$0.3 \div 0.01 = \dfrac{0.3}{0.01}$

$= \dfrac{0.3 \times 100}{0.01 \times 100}$

$= \dfrac{30}{1}$

$0.01\overline{)0.3}$ ➡ $1\overline{)30} = 30$

$0.3 \div 0.001 = \dfrac{0.3}{0.001}$

$= \dfrac{0.3 \times 100}{0.001 \times 100}$

$= \dfrac{300}{1}$

$0.001\overline{)0.3}$ ➡ $1\overline{)300} = 300$

1. Divide.
   (a) 500 ÷ 0.1
   (b) 500 ÷ 0.01
   (c) 500 ÷ 0.001
   (d) 50 ÷ 0.1
   (e) 50 ÷ 0.01
   (f) 50 ÷ 0.001
   (g) 5 ÷ 0.1
   (h) 5 ÷ 0.01
   (i) 5 ÷ 0.001
   (j) 0.5 ÷ 0.1
   (k) 0.5 ÷ 0.01
   (l) 0.5 ÷ 0.001
   (m) 0.05 ÷ 0.1
   (n) 0.05 ÷ 0.01
   (o) 0.05 ÷ 0.001
   (p) 0.005 ÷ 0.1
   (q) 0.005 ÷ 0.01
   (r) 0.005 ÷ 0.001

2. Estimate the values.
   (a) 4598 ÷ 3
        4598 ÷ 3 ≈ 4500 ÷ 3
               = ◻

   (b) 4598 ÷ 0.3
        4598 ÷ 0.3 ≈ 4500 ÷ 0.3
                  = 45,000 ÷ 3
                  = ◻

   (c) 45.98 ÷ 0.3
        45.98 ÷ 0.3 ≈ 45.0,0 ÷ 0.3
                   = 450 ÷ 3
                   = ◻

   (d) 4.598 ÷ 0.03
        4.598 ÷ 0.03 ≈ 4.500 ÷ 0.03
                    = 450 ÷ 3
                    = ◻

3. (a) Estimate the value of 5.94 ÷ 0.7.
        5.94 ÷ 0.7 = 59.4 ÷ 7
                   ≈ 56 ÷ 7
                   = ◻

   (b) Find the value of 5.94 ÷ 0.7 correct to 2 decimal places.

```
                                              8.4              8.485...
   0.7) 5.94   ➡   7) 59.4   ➡   7) 59.4   ➡   7) 59.400
                                   5 6              5 6
                                   ─────            ─────
                                   3 4              3 4
                                   2 8              2 8
                                   ─────            ─────
                                     6              6 0
                                                    5 6
                                                    ─────
                                                      4 0
                                                      3 5
                                                    ─────
                                                        5
                                                        ⋮
```

   5.94 ÷ 0.7 ≈ ◻   OR

   5.94 ÷ 0.7 = 8.49 (correct to 2 decimal places)

4. Find the following correct to at most 2 decimal places.
   (a) 45.9 ÷ 0.3
   (b) 89.98 ÷ 0.04
   (c) 100 ÷ 0.008

Exercise 17, pages 27 - 28

5. Estimate the values.

(a) $3687 \div 42$
$3687 \div 42 \approx 3600 \div 40$
$= \boxed{}$

(b) $3687 \div 4.2$
$3687 \div 4.2 \approx 3600 \div 4$
$= \boxed{}$

(c) $3687 \div 0.42$
$3687 \div 0.42 \approx 3600 \div 0.4$
$= 36{,}000 \div 4$
$= \boxed{}$

(d) $36.87 \div 4.2$
$36.87 \div 4.2 \approx 36 \div 4$
$= \boxed{}$

(e) $36.87 \div 0.042$
$36.87 \div 0.042 \approx 36 \div 0.04$
$= 3600 \div 4$
$= \boxed{}$

6. (a) Estimate the value of $128.7 \div 0.24$.
$128.7 \div 0.24 \approx 120 \div 0.2$
$= 1200 \div 2$
$= \boxed{}$

(b) Find the value of $128.7 \div 0.24$ correct to 2 decimal places.

```
              536            536.25
0.24)128.7   24)12870    24)12870    24)12870.00
            → 24)12870    →   120     →    120
                            ─────          ─────
                              87             87
                              72             72
                            ─────          ─────
                             150            150
                             144            144
                            ─────          ─────
                               6             60
                                             48
                                           ─────
                                            120
                                            120
                                           ─────
                                              0
```

$128.7 \div 0.24 = \boxed{}$

7. Find the following correct to at most 2 decimal places.

(a) $45.9 \div 1.8$ (b) $42.98 \div 0.16$ (c) $15 \div 0.006$

Exercise 18, page 29

PRACTICE B

Find the value of each of the following:

	(a)	(b)	(c)
1.	10 × 5.7	100 × 1.508	7.25 × 1000
2.	30 × 0.002	400 × 3.29	6.8 × 3000
3.	84 × 0.13	56 × 2.07	1.29 × 29
4.	39 ÷ 10	34.2 ÷ 100	9 ÷ 1000
5.	99 ÷ 30	648 ÷ 600	60 ÷ 2000

6. Divide.

   (a) 256.8 ÷ 24   (b) 96.82 ÷ 47   (c) 15 ÷ 12

7. Estimate the value of each of the following:

   (a) 0.398 × 41   (b) 7.192 × 89   (c) 49.97 × 38
   (d) 6.254 ÷ 72   (e) 33.14 ÷ 58   (f) 375.23 ÷ 69

8. Find the value of each of the following:

   (a) 45.6 × 0.1   (b) 3.9 × 0.01   (c) 0.32 × 0.1
   (d) 9.2 ÷ 0.001   (e) 36 ÷ 0.01   (f) 0.32 ÷ 0.1

9. What is the missing number in each ▢ ?

   (a) 1 = ▢ × 10   (b) 0.1 × ▢ = 100

   (c) 0.1 × ▢ = 0.001   (d) 0.01 ÷ ▢ = 100

   (e) 10 = ▢ ÷ 0.01   (f) 0.1 ÷ ▢ = 1000

10. Estimate the values, and then give the answers correct to
    1 decimal place.

    (a) 9.45 × 0.5   (b) 0.34 × 5.02   (c) 80.4 × 1.6
    (d) 4.59 ÷ 0.3   (e) 0.43 ÷ 0.21   (f) 38 ÷ 0.012

REVIEW 7

1. Round 24,582,000 to the nearest hundred thousand.

2. What is the missing number in each ☐?

   (a) $9.08 = 9 +$ ☐

   (b) $8.602 = 8 + 0.6 +$ ☐

   (c) $23.38 = 20 + 3 +$ ☐ $+ 0.08$

   (d) $1.909 = 1 + \dfrac{☐}{10} + \dfrac{9}{1000}$

3. Round each number to the nearest whole number.
   (a) 8.9   (b) 8.07   (c) 0.899   (d) 109.5

4. Fill in the missing numbers.

   (a) $(3 \times 7) + (0.4 \times 7) = $ ☐ $\times 7$

   (b) $(400 \times 0.9) - (3 \times 0.9) = $ ☐ $\times 0.9$

5. Arrange the numbers in decreasing order.

   (a) 1.09   1.03 $\dfrac{1}{6}$ $\dfrac{1}{16}$ (b) 3.022   3.22   3.202   3.2

6. Express each decimal as a fraction in its simplest form.
   (a) 0.6   (b) 4.40   (c) 6.105   (d) 7.225

7. Express each fraction as a decimal.

   (a) $4\dfrac{7}{10}$ (b) $6\dfrac{9}{100}$ (c) $8\dfrac{12}{25}$ (d) $2\dfrac{9}{50}$

8. What is the missing number in each ☐?

   (a) $3.5 \times$ ☐ $= 35$ (b) $3.72 \times$ ☐ $= 372$

   (c) $62 \times$ ☐ $= 0.062$ (d) $1.5 \times$ ☐ $= 0.015$

9. Find the prime factorization of
   (a) 150   (b) 96

10. Estimate, and then find the actual value.
    (a) 0.39×6.7 (b) 12.08×3.8 (c) 47.86×0.57
    (d) $3.42 \div 38$ (e) $52.05 \div 2.5$ (f) $4.07 \div 0.74$

11. Find the value of each of the following in its simplest form.

    (a) $\frac{5}{8} \times \frac{7}{10}$ (b) $\frac{5}{8} \div 2$ (c) $\frac{8}{5} \div \frac{4}{3}$

12. Find the area of the shaded part of each rectangle.

    (a)

    9.2 cm, 4 cm

    (b)

    8 cm, 3 cm, 10 cm

13. 48 out of 112 members of a club are women. What fraction of the members are women?

14. There are 36 marbles in a box. 8 of them are blue and the rest are red. What is the ratio of the number of red marbles to the number of blue marbles? Give the answer in its simplest form.

15. Josh bought a motorcycle. He paid a deposit of $210 and 10 monthly installments of $31.25 each. Find the cost of the motorcycle.

16. Mrs. Garcia bought 2.5 kg of sugar. She used 325 g of it to make cookies and 1.45 kg to make cakes. How much sugar did she have left? Give the answer in kilograms.

17. Susan bought 10 apples and 8 pears. The apples cost $0.35 each. A pear cost twice as much as an apple. How much did she pay altogether?

18. Henry bought 1 liter of fruit juice. He kept $\frac{1}{4}$ liter of it in a bottle and poured the remainder equally into 6 cups. How much fruit juice was there in each cup? Give the answer in liters.

Review 7, pages 30 - 33

8 MEASURES AND VOLUMES

1 Conversion of Measures

The table shows the heights of 3 boys in meters. Express the heights in centimeters.

Name	Height
Sam	1.4 m
Ryan	1.26 m
Matthew	1.32 m

1 m = 100 cm

0.1 m = 10 cm

0.01 m = 1 cm

0.4 m = 40 cm

1.4 m = 100 cm + 40 cm

= 140 cm

Sam's height is 140 cm.

Ryan's height is ⬜ cm.

Matthew's height is ⬜ cm.

1. (a) Express 0.75 m in centimeters.
   0.75 m = 0.75 × 100 cm

   = ☐ cm

   (b) Express 3.75 m in centimeters.

   3.75 m = 3.75 × 100 cm

   = ☐ cm

   (c) Express 0.5 ft in inches.

   0.5 ft = 0.5 × 12 in.

   = ☐ in.

1 m = 100 cm
1 km = 1000 m
1 yd = 3 ft
1 ft = 12 in.
1 kg = 1000 g
1 lb = 16 oz
1 ℓ = 1000 ml
1 gal = 4 qt
1 qt = 2 pt
1 qt = 4 c

2. (a) Express 2.8 kg in grams.   (b) Express 6.25 lb in ounces.

   2.8 kg = 2.8 × 1000 g   6.25 lb = 6.25 × 16 oz

   = ☐ g   = ☐ oz

3. Find the equivalent measures.

   (a) 0.6 m = ☐ cm   (b) 0.49 ℓ = ☐ ml

   (c) 0.615 km = ☐ m   (d) 0.3 kg = ☐ g

   (e) 1.85 kg = ☐ g   (f) 4.2 ℓ = ☐ ml

   (g) 2.75 qt = ☐ c   (h) 3.5 lb = ☐ oz

   (i) 3.25 ft = ☐ in.   (j) 0.5 gal = ☐ qt

4. Express 4.2 ℓ in liters and milliliters.

   4.2 ℓ = 4 ℓ ☐ ml   0.2 ℓ = 0.2 × 1000 ml

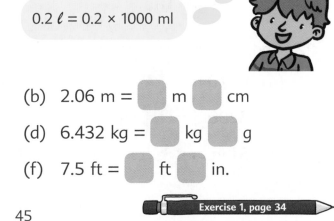

5. Find the equivalent measures.

   (a) 3.45 km = ☐ km ☐ m   (b) 2.06 m = ☐ m ☐ cm

   (c) 4.005 ℓ = ☐ ℓ ☐ ml   (d) 6.432 kg = ☐ kg ☐ g

   (e) 4.25 lb = ☐ lb ☐ oz   (f) 7.5 ft = ☐ ft ☐ in.

Exercise 1, page 34

6. Express 145 ml in liters.

   $145 \text{ ml} = \dfrac{145}{1000} \ell$

   $\phantom{145 \text{ ml}} = \boxed{} \ell$

   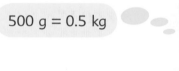

7. Find the equivalent measures.

   (a) 350 m = $\boxed{}$ km   (b) 420 ml = $\boxed{}$ ℓ

   (c) 625 g = $\boxed{}$ kg   (d) 30 cm = $\boxed{}$ m

8. (a) Use a tape measure to find your friend's height in meters and centimeters.
   (b) Express the height in meters.

9. Express 3 kg 500 g in kilograms.

   3 kg 500 g = 3 kg + 0.5 kg   500 g = 0.5 kg

   $\phantom{3 \text{ kg } 500 \text{ g}} = \boxed{}$ kg

10. Find the equivalent measures.

    (a) 4 m 35 cm = $\boxed{}$ m   (b) 5 km 90 m = $\boxed{}$ km

    (c) 2 ℓ 800 ml = $\boxed{}$ ℓ (d) 4 kg 75 g = $\boxed{}$ kg

    (e) 3 ft 9 in. = $\boxed{}$ ft   (f) 3 qt 2 c = $\boxed{}$ qt

11. Express 3080 g in kilograms.   3080.0

    Method 1:   **Method 2:**

    3080 g = 3 kg 80 g $3080 \text{ g} = \dfrac{3080}{1000}$ kg

    $\phantom{3080 \text{ g}} = \boxed{}$ kg $\phantom{3080 \text{ g}} = \boxed{}$ kg

12. Find the equivalent measures.

    (a) 4070 m = $\boxed{}$ km   (b) 2380 ml = $\boxed{}$ ℓ

    (c) 5200 g = $\boxed{}$ kg   (d) 605 cm = $\boxed{}$ m

    (e) 51 in. = $\boxed{}$ ft   (f) 88 oz = $\boxed{}$ lb

Exercise 2, pages 35 - 36

Find the equivalent measures.

1. (a) 0.258 ℓ = ☐ ml   (b) 0.75 gal = ☐ qt

   (c) 0.085 km = ☐ m   (d) 0.25 ft = ☐ in.

   (e) 0.706 kg = ☐ g   (f) 0.5 lb = ☐ oz

2. (a) 670 ml = ☐ ℓ   (b) 12 oz = ☐ lb

   (c) 105 m = ☐ km   (d) 3 c = ☐ qt

   (e) 69 g = ☐ kg   (f) 6 in. = ☐ ft

3. (a) 20.08 km = ☐ km ☐ m   (b) 3.75 qt = ☐ qt ☐ c

   (c) 16.5 ℓ = ☐ ℓ ☐ ml   (d) 18.5 ft = ☐ ft ☐ in.

   (e) 2.08 kg = ☐ kg ☐ g   (f) 4.75 lb = ☐ lb ☐ oz

4. (a) 9 m 60 cm = ☐ m   (b) 6 gal 3 qt = ☐ qt

   (c) 4 ℓ 705 ml = ☐ ℓ   (d) 2 lb 5 oz = ☐ oz

   (e) 25 km 6 m = ☐ km   (f) 3 ft 7 in. = ☐ in.

5. Write >, <, or = in each ◯.

   (a) 950 ml ◯ 1 ℓ   (b) 2.038 km ◯ 38 m

   (c) 0.09 m ◯ 9 cm   (d) 3.5 ℓ ◯ 3 ℓ 5 ml

   (e) 1.25 kg ◯ 1 kg 25 g   (f) 10.08 kg ◯ 10 kg 80 g

   (g) 82 in. ◯ 7 ft   (h) 6.5 lb ◯ 104 oz

6. Juliana is 1.64 m tall. Her sister is 6 cm shorter. Find her sister's height in meters.

7. Rachel had 3.54 kg of flour. She used 250 g to make cookies and 1.25 kg to bake cakes. How many kilograms of flour did she have left?

2 Volume of Rectangular Prisms

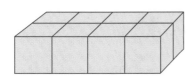

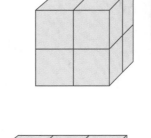

The **volume** of a solid is the amount of space it occupies.

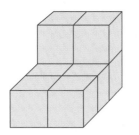

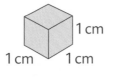

These solids have the same volume.
The volume of each solid is 8 cubic units.

The volume of a unit cube is 1 **cubic unit**.

Each edge of the cube is 1 cm long.
The volume of the cube is 1 **cubic centimeter (cm³)**.

1 cm
1 cm   1 cm

The cubic centimeter (cm³) is a unit of volume.

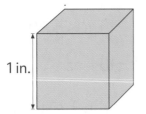

1 in.

We can also use other cubic measures, such as the cubic inch (in.³), cubic foot (ft³) or cubic meter (m³).

1. The following solids are made up of 1-cm cubes. Find the volume of each solid.

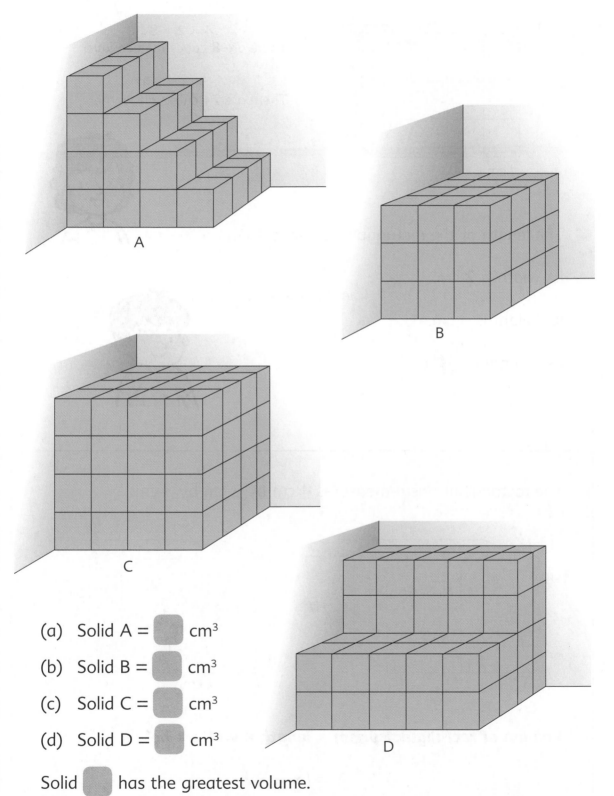

A

B

C

D

(a) Solid A = ☐ cm³

(b) Solid B = ☐ cm³

(c) Solid C = ☐ cm³

(d) Solid D = ☐ cm³

Solid ☐ has the greatest volume.

2. The rectangular prism is made up of 1-cm cubes.

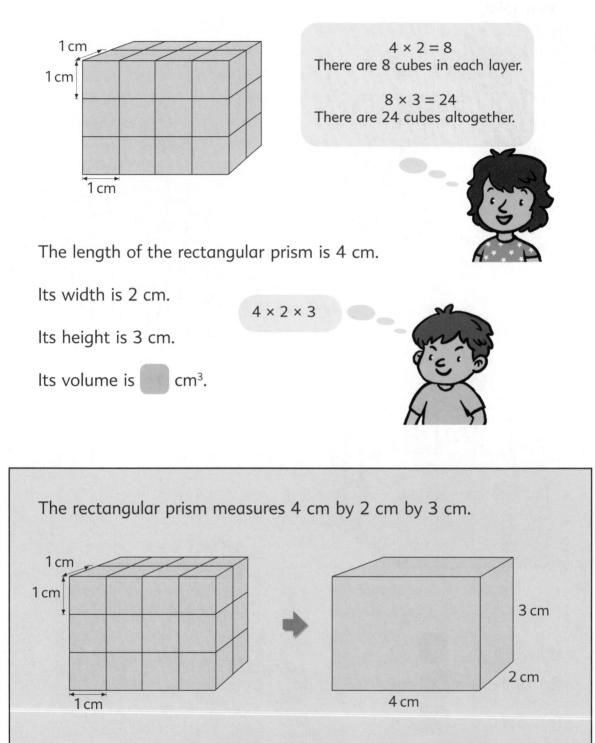

4 × 2 = 8
There are 8 cubes in each layer.

8 × 3 = 24
There are 24 cubes altogether.

The length of the rectangular prism is 4 cm.

Its width is 2 cm.

4 × 2 × 3

Its height is 3 cm.

Its volume is ▢ cm³.

The rectangular prism measures 4 cm by 2 cm by 3 cm.

Volume of rectangular prism = length × width × height

$$V = l \times w \times h$$

3. Find the volume of the rectangular prism which measures 5 cm by 2 cm by 3 cm.

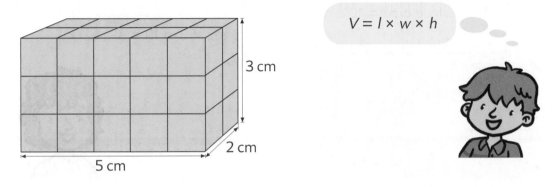

$$V = l \times w \times h$$

3 cm

2 cm

5 cm

Volume of the rectangular prism = $5 \times 2 \times 3 = \boxed{}$ cm³

4. Find the volume of each rectangular prism.

(a)

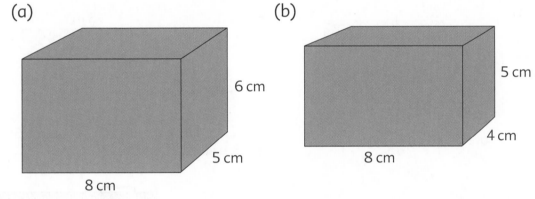

6 cm

5 cm

8 cm

(b)

5 cm

4 cm

8 cm

5. Find the volume of each cube.

(a)

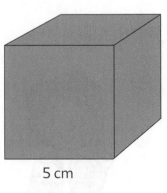

5 cm

(b)

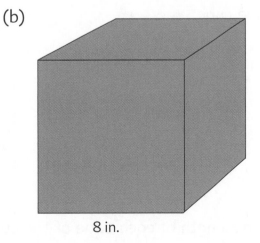

8 in.

6. The top surface area of the rectangular prism is 10 cm². The height of the rectangular prism is 3 cm. Find its volume.

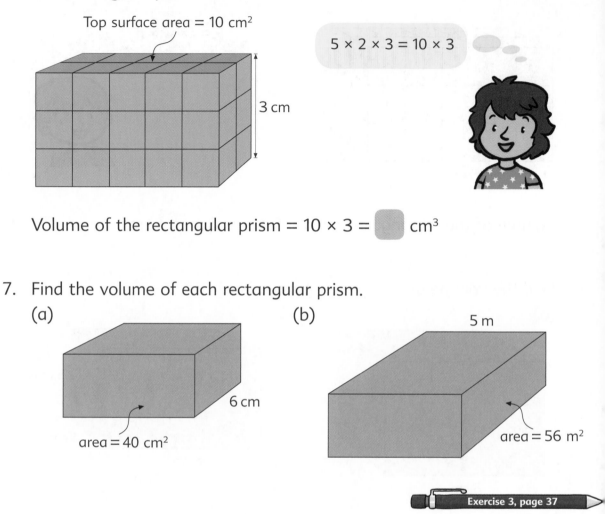

Top surface area = 10 cm²

3 cm

$5 \times 2 \times 3 = 10 \times 3$

Volume of the rectangular prism = $10 \times 3 = \boxed{}$ cm³

7. Find the volume of each rectangular prism.

(a)

6 cm

area = 40 cm²

(b)

5 m

area = 56 m²

Exercise 3, page 37

8. The volume of a cube is 27 cm³. Find the length of one edge of the cube.

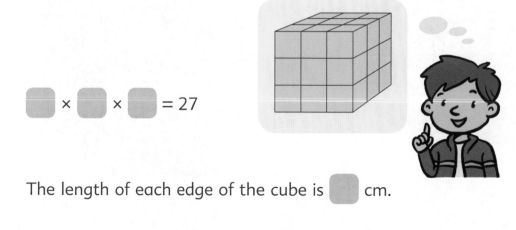

$\boxed{} \times \boxed{} \times \boxed{} = 27$

The length of each edge of the cube is $\boxed{}$ cm.

9. The volume of a rectangular prism is 24 cm³. The length of the rectangular prism is 3 cm and its width is 2 cm. Find its height.

$V = l \times w \times h$

$h = V \div (l \times w)$

$\quad = \dfrac{V}{l \times w}$

$\quad = \dfrac{24}{3 \times 2}$

$\quad = \boxed{}$ cm

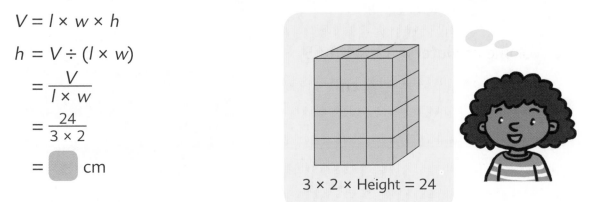

$3 \times 2 \times \text{Height} = 24$

10. Find the unknown edge of each rectangular prism.

(a)

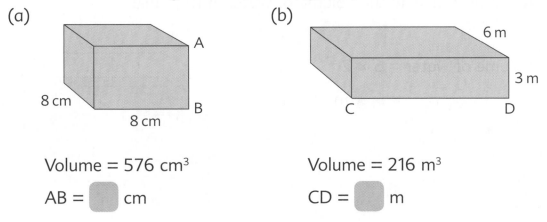

8 cm

8 cm

A

B

Volume = 576 cm³

AB = ☐ cm

(b)

6 m

3 m

C   D

Volume = 216 m³

CD = ☐ m

11. Find the unknown edge of each rectangular prism.

(a)

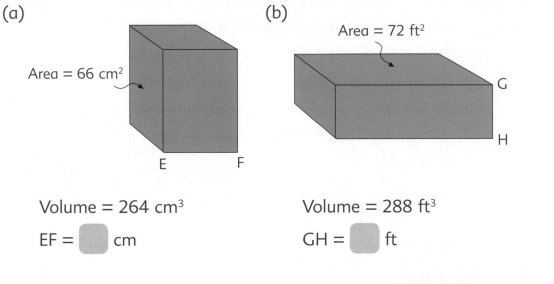

Area = 66 cm²

E   F

Volume = 264 cm³

EF = ☐ cm

(b)

Area = 72 ft²

G

H

Volume = 288 ft³

GH = ☐ ft

Exercise 4, page 38

12. A rectangular container, 12 cm long and 10 cm wide, is filled with water to a depth of 5 cm. Find the volume of water in the container.

Volume of water = 12 × 10 × 5

    = ⬚ cm³

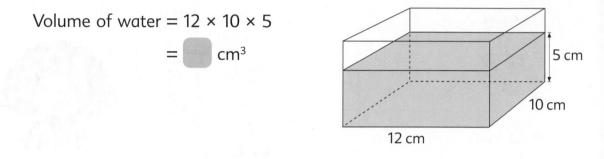

5 cm

10 cm

12 cm

13. A rectangular tank has a base area of 6 m². It contains water to a depth of 2 m. Find the volume of water in the tank.

Volume of water = 6 × 2

    = ⬚ m³

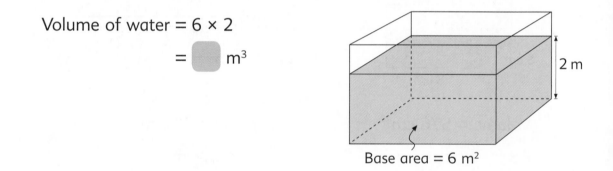

2 m

Base area = 6 m²

14. A rectangular container, 8 cm long and 5 cm wide, contains 120 cm³ of water. Find the height of the water level in the container.

Height of water level = $\dfrac{120}{8 \times 5}$

    = ⬚ cm

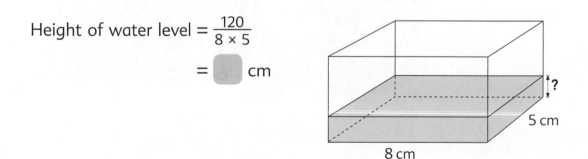

?

5 cm

8 cm

15. The plastic box measures 10 cm by 10 cm by 10 cm.
It can hold 1 liter of water.

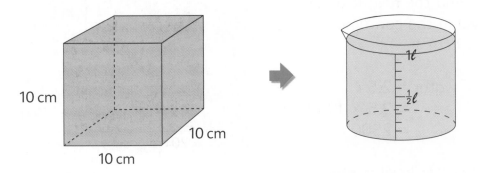

Maximum volume of water that the box can contain = 10 × 10 × 10

= ☐ cm³

1 ℓ = ☐ cm³

1 ml = ☐ cm³

1 ℓ = 1000 ml

16. (a) Express 2.5 liters in cubic centimeters.

2.5 ℓ = 2.5 × 1000 cm³

= ☐ cm³

1 ℓ = 1000 cm³

(b) Express 3200 cm³ in liters.

$3200 \text{ cm}^3 = \frac{3200}{1000} \ell$

= ☐ ℓ

17. A rectangular tank measures
40 cm by 25 cm by 30 cm. How
many liters of water are in the tank
when it is full? (1 ℓ = 1000 cm³)

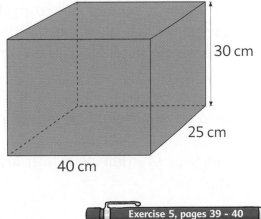

Volume of water = 40 × 25 × 30

= ☐ cm³

= ☐ ℓ

55

Exercise 5, pages 39 - 40

18. A rectangular container, 20 cm long and 10 cm wide, contains 2.5 liters of water. Find the height of the water level in the container.
($1\,\ell = 1000\ cm^3$)

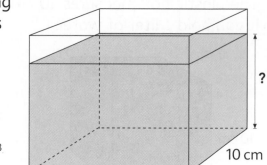

Volume of water = 2.5 ℓ
$$= 2.5 \times 1000\ cm^3$$
$$= 2500\ cm^3$$

Height of water level = $\dfrac{2500}{20 \times 10}$

$$= \boxed{}\ cm$$

19. A rectangular tank measuring 25 cm by 16 cm by 30 cm is filled with water to a depth of 12 cm. How much more water is needed to fill the tank? Give your answer in milliliters.

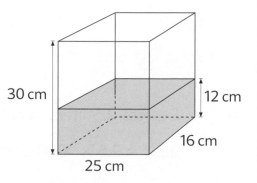

Increase in height of water level
$= 30 - 12$
$= 18$ cm

Volume of water needed = $25 \times 16 \times 18 = \boxed{}\ cm^3 = \boxed{}$ milliliters.

20. A rectangular container measuring 20 cm by 10 cm by 10 cm is filled with water to its brim. If 0.75 liters of water is poured out from the container, what will be the height of the water level left in the container?

Decrease in height of water level = $\dfrac{750}{20 \times 10} = \boxed{}$ cm

Height of remaining water level = $10 - \boxed{} = \boxed{}$ cm

Exercise 6, pages 41 - 42

1. Find the unknown edge of each rectangular prism.

   (a)

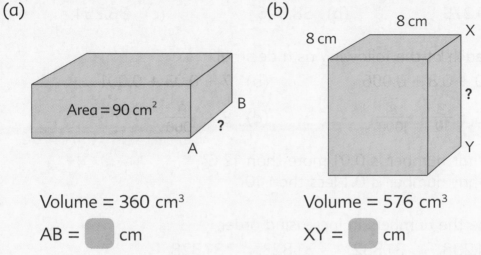

   Volume = 360 cm³

   AB = ⬤ cm

   (b)

   Volume = 576 cm³

   XY = ⬤ cm

2. Find the volume of water in each container. Give the answers in liters.
   (1 ℓ = 1000 cm³)

   (a)

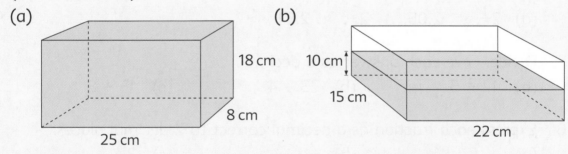

   (b)

3. The volume of a cube is 125 cm³.
   Find the length of each edge of the cube.

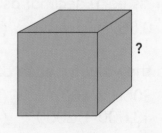

4. A rectangular tank, 12 m long and 5 m
   wide, contains 300 m³ of water when it
   is full. Find the height of the tank.

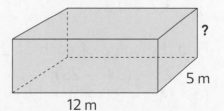

REVIEW 8

1. What is the value of the digit 5 in each of the following?
    (a) 10.275   (b) 58,026   (c) 36.254

2. Write each of the following as a decimal.
    (a) 50 + 0.8 + 0.006   (b) 7 + 0.03 + 0.001
    (c) $45 + \frac{3}{10} + \frac{8}{1000}$ (d) $8 + \frac{9}{1000}$

3. (a) What number is 0.01 more than 12.6?
    (b) What number is 0.1 less than 10?

4. Arrange the numbers in increasing order.
    (a) 31,238,   31,832,   31,823,   31,328
    (b) $4\frac{1}{6}$, $\frac{9}{2}$, $4\frac{2}{5}$, $4\frac{3}{10}$
    (c) 4.98,   4.089,   498,   4809
    (d) $2\frac{1}{2}$,   2.05, $2\frac{3}{5}$,   2.51

5. Divide. Give each answer as a decimal.
    (a) 42 ÷ 5   (b) 23 ÷ 4   (c) 15 ÷ 8

6. Express each fraction as a decimal correct to 2 decimal places.
    (a) $\frac{3}{7}$ (b) $\frac{2}{9}$ (c) $3\frac{5}{6}$

7. Express each decimal as a fraction in its simplest form.
    (a) 0.062   (b) 2.36   (c) 6.308

8. Find the value of each of the following.
    (a) 3000 × 400   (b) 6.04 × 3000   (c) 3.25 × 62
    (d) 48,000 ÷ 2000   (e) 48.9 ÷ 100   (f) 6.5 ÷ 2
    (g) 34 × 0.4   (h) 4.5 × 6.2   (i) 1.26 × 0.31
    (j) 3.7 ÷ 0.2   (k) 45.6 ÷ 12   (l) 0.657 ÷ 0.18

9. Find the value of each of the following.
    (a) 23 × (34 − 25)   (b) 7 × 8 + 48 ÷ 3
    (c) (45 − 31) × 4 + 12   (d) (28 + 9) × (12 − 7)

10. Find the value of each of the following in its simplest form.

(a) $\frac{2}{3} \times 45$ (b) $\frac{35}{12} \times \frac{18}{7}$ (c) $\frac{7}{9} \div 5$

(d) $4 \div \frac{3}{8}$ (e) $\frac{3}{5} \div \frac{5}{8}$ (f) $\frac{14}{3} \times \frac{1}{7}$

11. Find the prime factorization of 124.

12. Mrs. Cohen bought 15 m of string. She used 2.5 m to tie a package. Then, she cut the remainder into 6 equal pieces. Find the length of each piece. Give the answer in meters correct to 1 decimal place.

13. Mrs. Smith used $\frac{3}{8}$ of a bag of flour to bake cakes and $\frac{1}{5}$ of the remainder to bake biscuits. What fraction of the flour did she use altogether?

14. Mr. Venezia sold $\frac{1}{3}$ of his eggs in the morning and $\frac{1}{4}$ in the afternoon. He had 320 eggs left. How many eggs did he have at first?

15. The ratio of the number of female members to the number of male members in a club is 3 : 5. If there are 48 female members, how many members are there altogether?

16. The area of a rectangle is 300 m². If the length of the rectangle is 20 m, find its width and perimeter.

17. Find the perimeter and area of the figure.
(All lines meet at right angles.)

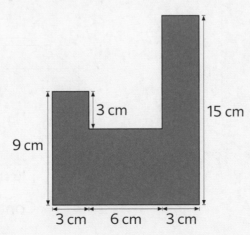

59

18. Find the area of the shaded figure.

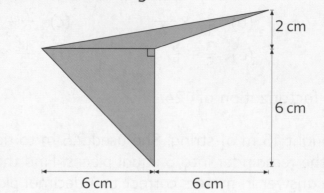

19. Find the volume of each rectangular prism.

(a)

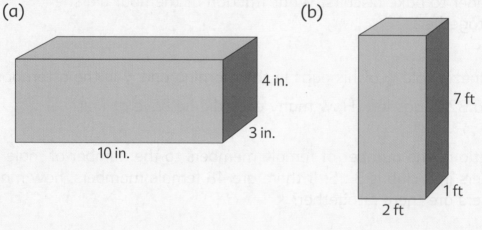

(b)

20. Container A was filled with water to its brim. Container B was empty. All the water in Container A is poured into Container B. What is the height of the water level in Container B now?

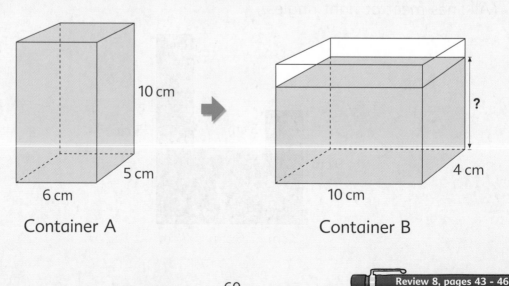

Container A

Container B

9 PERCENTAGE

1 Percent

There are 100 seats in a theater. 55 seats are occupied.

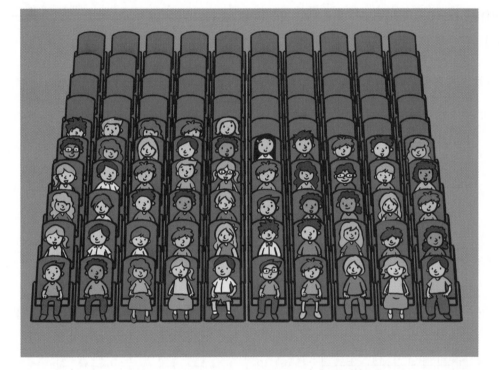

55% of the seats are occupied.

We read 55% as **55 percent**.

55% means **55 out of 100**.

55% is another way of writing $\frac{55}{100}$ or 0.55.

1. 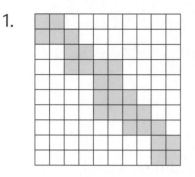   The whole is divided into 100 equal parts.
27 parts are shaded.
What **percentage** of the whole is shaded?

27 out of 100 is ☐ %.

2. What percentage of the whole is shaded?

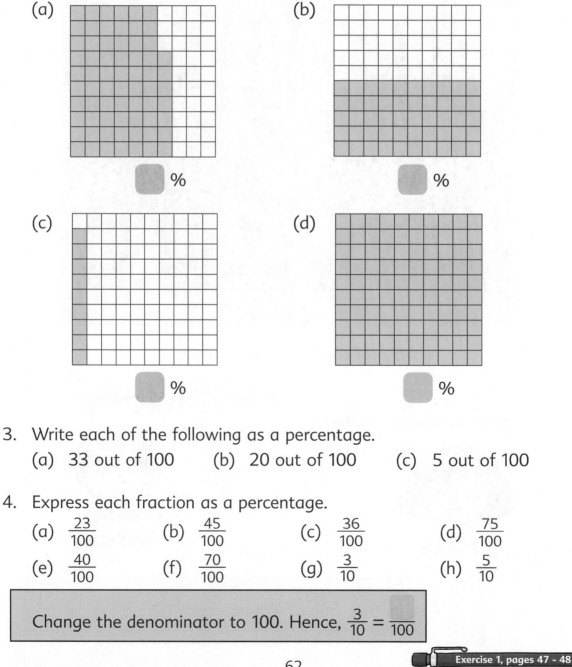

(a)   ☐ %

(b)   ☐ %

(c)   ☐ %

(d)   ☐ %

3. Write each of the following as a percentage.
   (a) 33 out of 100   (b) 20 out of 100   (c) 5 out of 100

4. Express each fraction as a percentage.
   (a) $\frac{23}{100}$ (b) $\frac{45}{100}$ (c) $\frac{36}{100}$ (d) $\frac{75}{100}$
   (e) $\frac{40}{100}$ (f) $\frac{70}{100}$ (g) $\frac{3}{10}$ (h) $\frac{5}{10}$

Change the denominator to 100. Hence, $\frac{3}{10} = \frac{}{100}$

62

Exercise 1, pages 47 - 48

5. Express 0.35 as a percentage.

$$0.35 = \frac{35}{100}$$

$$= \boxed{} \%$$

6. Express each decimal as a percentage.
   (a) 0.07   (b) 0.02   (c) 0.85   (d) 0.7

7. Express 43% as a decimal.

$$43\% = \frac{43}{100}$$

$$= \boxed{}$$

Write $\frac{43}{100}$ as a decimal.

8. Express each percentage as a decimal.
   (a) 28%   (b) 88%   (c) 30%   (d) 5%

9.

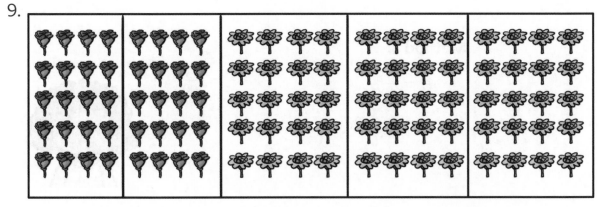

40% of the flowers are roses. What fraction of the flowers are roses?

$$40\% = \frac{40}{100}$$

$$= \boxed{}$$

Write $\frac{40}{100}$ in its simplest form.

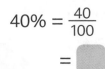 of the flowers are roses.

10. Express each percentage as a fraction in its simplest form.
   (a) 10%   (b) 80%   (c) 25%   (d) 75%
   (e) 5%   (f) 8%   (g) 4%   (h) 2%

Exercise 2, pages 49 - 51

② Writing Fractions as Percentages

Mr. Goldberg has painted $\frac{3}{4}$ of a wall.

What percentage of the wall has he painted?

Method 1:

$$\frac{3}{4} = \frac{75}{100}$$

$$= \boxed{} \%$$

Method 2:

$$\frac{3}{4} = \frac{3}{4} \times 100\%$$

$$= \boxed{} \%$$

1 whole is 100%.

$\frac{3}{4}$ is $\frac{3}{4}$ of 100%.

He has painted ☐ % of the wall.

1. Express each fraction as a percentage.

   (a)

   $\frac{2}{5} = \frac{4}{10} = $ ⬚ %

   (b)

   $\frac{1}{2} = \frac{5}{10} = $ ⬚ %

2. Express 7 out of 25 as a percentage.

   Method 1 :

   $\frac{7}{25} = \frac{28}{100} = $ ⬚ %

   Method 2:

   $\frac{7}{25} = \frac{7}{25} \times 100\% = $ ⬚ %

3. Limei has 20 apples. 14 of them are red apples. What percentage of the apples are red apples?

   $\frac{14}{20} = $ ⬚ %

   $\frac{14}{20}$ is 14 out of 20.

   ⬚ % of the apples are red apples.

4. Express each fraction as a percentage.

   (a) $\frac{1}{4}$

   (b) $\frac{2}{5}$

   (c) $\frac{4}{5}$

   (d) $\frac{9}{20}$

   (e) $\frac{13}{20}$

   (f) $\frac{6}{25}$

   (g) $\frac{14}{25}$

   (h) $\frac{41}{50}$

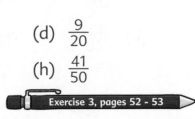Exercise 3, pages 52 - 53

5. Express 180 out of 300 as a percentage.

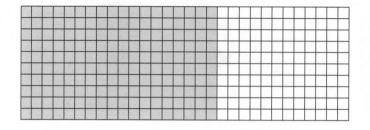

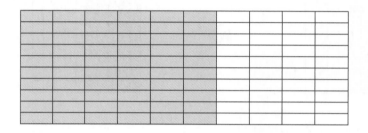

Method 1:

$$\frac{180}{300} = \frac{60}{100} = \boxed{}\%$$

Method 2:

$$\frac{180}{300} = \frac{180}{300} \times 100\% = \boxed{}\%$$

6. 200 children are at a concert. 98 of them are boys. What percentage of the children are boys?

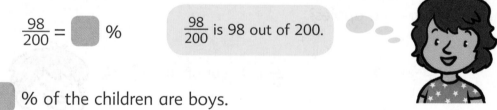

$$\frac{98}{200} = \boxed{}\%$$

$\frac{98}{200}$ is 98 out of 200.

$\boxed{}$ % of the children are boys.

7. Express each fraction as a percentage.

(a) $\frac{8}{200}$ (b) $\frac{36}{200}$ (c) $\frac{60}{300}$ (d) $\frac{129}{300}$

(e) $\frac{40}{400}$ (f) $\frac{128}{400}$ (g) $\frac{20}{500}$ (h) $\frac{255}{500}$

Exercise 4, pages 54 - 55

8. What percentage of each of the following bars is shaded? (Use the percentage scale to help you.)

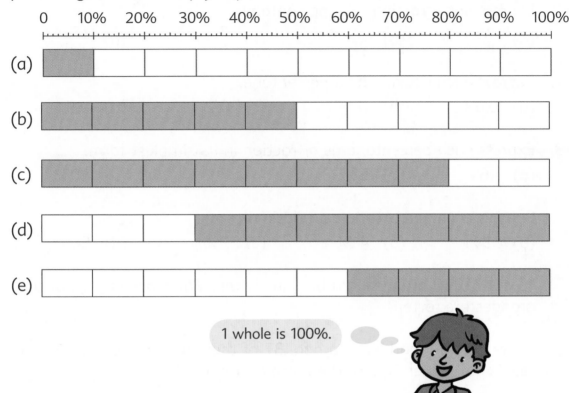

1 whole is 100%.

9. $\frac{3}{4}$ of the pies which Mrs. Goodman made were apple pies.

(a) What percentage of the pies were apple pies?

$\frac{3}{4} = \frac{3}{4} \times 100\% = 75\%$

[ ] % of the pies were apple pies.

(b) What percentage of the pies were not apple pies?

$100\% - 75\% =$ [ ] %

[ ] % of the pies were not apple pies.

10. 7 out of 25 children are boys.
(a) What percentage of the children are boys?
(b) What percentage of the children are girls?

11. Sam had $750. He spent $300 and saved the rest. What percentage of the money did he save?

Exercise 5, pages 56 - 57

1. Express each fraction as a percentage.
   (a) $\frac{5}{100}$ (b) $\frac{9}{25}$ (c) $\frac{3}{5}$ (d) $\frac{8}{160}$

2. Express each decimal as a percentage.
   (a) 0.63   (b) 0.05   (c) 0.2   (d) 0.5

3. Express each percentage as a fraction in its simplest form.
   (a) 46%   (b) 5%   (c) 7%   (d) 80%

4. Express each percentage as a decimal.
   (a) 15%   (b) 41%   (c) 9%   (d) 50%

5. 15 out of 100 oranges in a box are rotten. What percentage of the oranges are rotten?

6. There are 100 marbles in a bag. 37 of them are green. The rest are red. What percentage of the marbles are red?

7. A football team won 60% of its games. What fraction of the games did the foorball team win?

8. If 70% of a tank is filled with water. What percentage of the tank is not filled?

9. $\frac{4}{5}$ of the books in a library are fiction books. What percentage of the books are fiction books?

10. 14 out of 50 vehicles in a parking lot are motorcycles. What percentage of the vehicles are motorcycles?

11. 1500 people took part in a walkathon. 450 of them were school children. The rest were adults. What percentage of the participants were adults?

12. Tracy bought 5 kg of flour. She use 2 kg to make cookies and the rest to make pineapple tarts. What percentage of the flour did she use to make pineapple tarts?

3 Percentage of a Quantity

There were 500 people at a concert. 30% of them were children.
How many children were there at the concert?

Method 1:

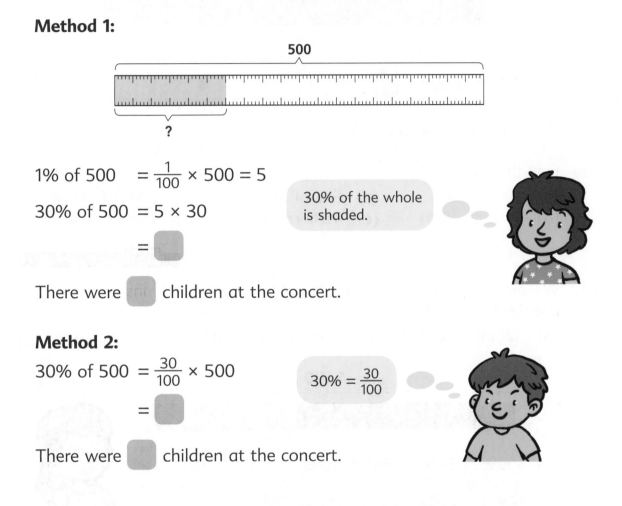

1% of 500 $= \frac{1}{100} \times 500 = 5$

30% of 500 $= 5 \times 30$

$= \boxed{}$

> 30% of the whole is shaded.

There were ⬚ children at the concert.

Method 2:

30% of 500 $= \frac{30}{100} \times 500$

$= \boxed{}$

> $30\% = \frac{30}{100}$

There were ⬚ children at the concert.

1. 120 students took part in a physical fitness test. 90% of them passed the test. How many students passed the test?

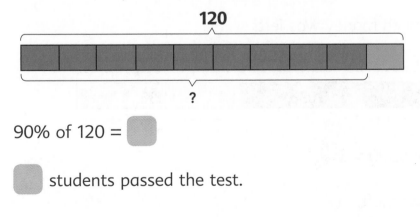

90% of 120 $= \boxed{}$

⬚ students passed the test.

2. Lindsey bought a refrigerator which cost $800. She had to pay 3% sales tax on $800. How much was the sales tax?

$800

3%	
?	

3% of $800 = $⬜

The sales tax was ⬜.

3. Find the values.

(a) 5% of 300   (b) 8% of 200   (c) 20% of 50 kg
(d) 25% of 40 m   (e) 45% of 70 km   (f) 75% of 400 g

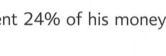 Exercise 6, pages 58 - 59

4. William had $500. He spent 24% of his money on transport and 36% on food.

(a) What percentage of his money was left?

$500

24%	36%	?

100% − 24% − 36% = 40%

⬜ % of his money was left.

 1 whole is 100%.

(b) How much money was left?

$500

24%	36%	40%

? (under 40%)

40% × $500 = $⬜

$⬜ was left.

5. There were 400 members in a swimming club. 12% of the members were children. The rest were adults. How many adults were there?

Method 1:

100% − 12% = 88%

88% of the members were adults.

88% × 400 = ▢

There were ▢ adults.

Method 2:

Number of children = 12% × 400 = 48

Number of adults = 400 − 48 = ▢

There were ▢ adults.

Exercise 7, pages 60 - 61

6. Ahmad has $2700 in a savings bank. The interest rate is 3% per year. How much money will he have in the bank after 1 year?

Find the interest for 1 year first.

Interest = 3% of $2700 = $▢

Amount of money in the bank after 1 year

= $2700 + Interest

= $▢

He will have $▢ in the bank after 1 year.

7. A man bought a refrigerator at a discount of 12%. Its usual price was $900. How much did he pay for the refrigerator?

Discount = $ ▢

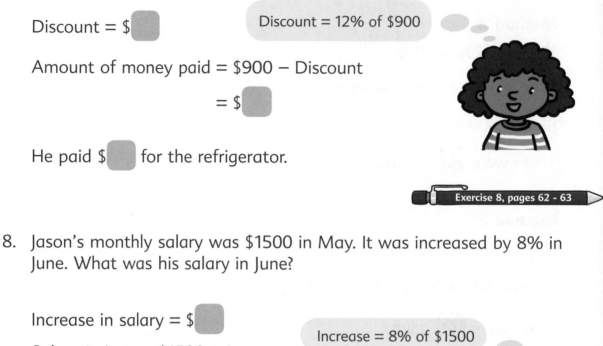

Discount = 12% of $900

Amount of money paid = $900 − Discount

= $ ▢

He paid $ ▢ for the refrigerator.

Exercise 8, pages 62 - 63

8. Jason's monthly salary was $1500 in May. It was increased by 8% in June. What was his salary in June?

Increase in salary = $ ▢

Salary in June = $1500 + Increase

Increase = 8% of $1500

= $ ▢

His salary in June was $ ▢ .

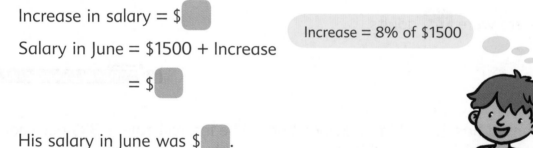

9. There were 400 members in a chess club last year. The membership was decreased by 5% this year. How many members are there this year?

Decrease = ▢

Decrease = 5% of 400

Number of members this year = 400 − Decrease

= ▢

There are ▢ members this year.

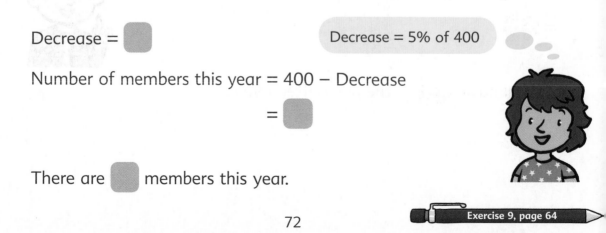

Exercise 9, page 64

1. Find the value of each of the following:
    (a) 8% of 82   (b) 40% of 308   (c) 62% of 520 m

2. The area of a garden is 60 m². 7% of it is taken up by a pond. What is the area of the pond?

3. There were 50 words in a spelling test. Sally spelled 90% of them correctly. How many words did she spell correctly?

4. There are 20 workers in a library. 55% of them are females. How many male workers are there?

5. Tasha earns $1350 monthly. She saves 30% of the money. How much does she save each month?

6. A swimming club had 720 members last year. This year the membership increased by 5%. Find the number of members this year.

7. Mary bought a swimsuit which cost $50. In addition, she had to pay 3% sales tax. How much did she pay for the swimsuit?

8. The usual price of a camera was $190. At a sale, it was sold at a discount of 30%. What was the sale price?

9. Mrs. Meier deposited $3500 in a bank. The bank paid 3% interest per year. How much money did she have in the bank after 1 year?

10. Travis shot 15 arrows. 40% of the arrows hit the target. How many arrows did not hit the target?

11. A library has a reading club. 30% of the members of the club are boys, 40% are girls and the rest are adults. If there are 280 members, how many of them are adults?

12. There are 200 spaces in a parking lot. 10% are for vans, 75% are for cars and the rest are for motorcycles. How many spaces are for motorcycles?

REVIEW 9

1. Round each of the following to 2 decimal places.

   (a) 7.275 km = ⬚ km

   (b) 3.005 kg = ⬚ kg

   (c) 0.279 ℓ = ⬚ ℓ

   (d) 30.455 cm = ⬚ cm

2. Write the following as a decimal.

   (a) 0.009 + 0.4 + 9 + 60

   (b) $\frac{9}{1000}$ + 7 + $\frac{8}{10}$ + 100

3. Express each fraction as a decimal correct to 1 decimal place.

   (a) $\frac{3}{4}$

   (b) $\frac{4}{9}$

   (c) $3\frac{1}{4}$

   (d) $3\frac{5}{8}$

4. Estimate, and then divide. Round each answer to 2 decimal places.

   (a) 34.92 ÷ 0.7

   (b) 45.6 ÷ 0.31

   (c) 928 ÷ 0.42

5. Write the prime factorization of 117.

6. Find the missing numbers.

   (a) (20 × 0.3) + (4 × 0.3) = ⬚ × 0.3

   (b) ($\frac{1}{2}$ × 4) + ($\frac{1}{2}$ × 6) = $\frac{1}{2}$ × ⬚

7. Multiply.

   (a) 3.43 × 40

   (b) 4.06 × 78

   (c) 21.5 × 0.45

8. Express the following using exponents.

   (a) 3 × 3 × 5 × 7 × 5

   (b) 13 × 11 × 11 × 2 × 7 × 2 × 2

9. Write the answer as a fraction in the simplest form.

   (a) $7\frac{3}{5} - 2\frac{1}{4}$

   (b) $6\frac{1}{3} + 8\frac{3}{5}$

   (c) $\frac{2}{3} \times \frac{4}{3}$

   (d) $\frac{4}{5} \div 3$

   (e) $\frac{7}{8} \div \frac{3}{2}$

   (f) $\frac{5}{6}$ of 120

10. Express 20 min as a fraction of 2 h.

11. Write each of the following as a percentage.

    (a) 14 out of 100

    (b) 6 out of 100

12. Express each fraction as a percentage.

(a) $\frac{15}{20}$ (b) $\frac{150}{200}$ (c) $\frac{260}{400}$

13. Find the value of each of the following.

(a) 3% of $60   (b) 10% of 450 g   (c) 35% of 120 m

14. A tank is $\frac{3}{5}$ filled with water. When 500 ml of water is poured out, the tank becomes $\frac{1}{2}$ full. Find the capacity of the tank in liters.

15. $\frac{3}{4}$ of a bag of beans weighs 4 kg. What is the weight of $\frac{1}{2}$ of the bag of beans in kilograms?

16. There are 200 families in an apartment complex. 186 of them own computers. What percentage of the families own computers?

17. A book costs $6. Sam sold it at a price 25% higher than the usual price. What was the selling price of the book?

18. The cost price of a bookcase was $180. It was sold at an amount 15% lower than the cost price. Find the selling price.

19. Container A is 24 cm long, 10 cm wide, and 40 cm high. It is $\frac{1}{4}$-filled with water. Container B is 30 cm long and 20 cm wide. It is filled with water to a height of 16 cm. When all the water in Container A is added to the water in Container B, Container B becomes $\frac{2}{3}$ full. What is the height of Container B?

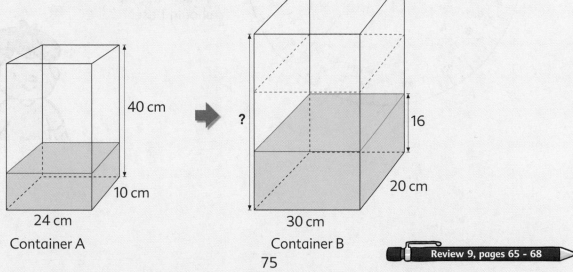

40 cm

10 cm

24 cm

Container A

?

16

20 cm

30 cm

Container B

Review 9, pages 65 - 68

10 ANGLES

1 Measuring Angles

What is the size of ∠m?

$$\angle m = 180° + 45°$$

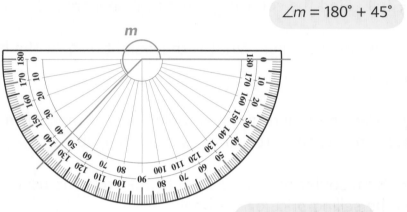

m

$$\angle m = 360° - 135°$$

Measure ∠n.

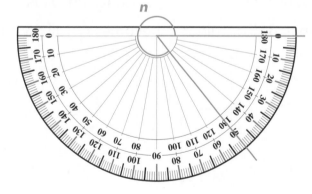

n

Which method should I use?

1. Estimate and then find each of the following marked angles by measurement.

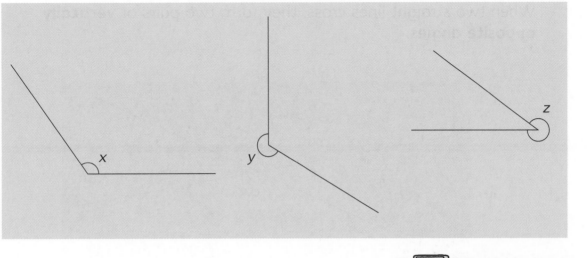

Exercice 1, pages 69 - 72

2.

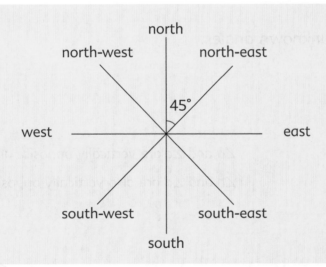

(a) You start facing north and turn clockwise to south-east. What angle do you turn through?

(b) You start facing west and turn counterclockwise to south-west. What angle do you turn through?

3. (a) You start facing north-west and turn clockwise through 90°. Which direction are you facing?

(b) After turning counterclockwise through 225°, you end up facing east. Which direction were you facing at the start?

Exercice 2, pages 73 - 74

② Finding Unknown Angles

When two straight lines cross, they form two pairs of **vertically opposite angles**.

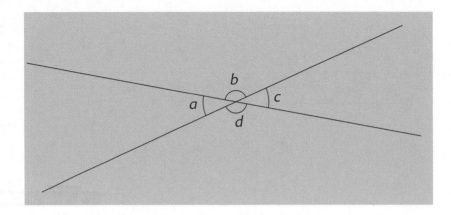

Measure the unknown angles.

$\angle a = 34°$

$\angle b = \boxed{}°$

$\angle c = \boxed{}°$

$\angle d = \boxed{}°$

$\angle a = \angle c$

$\angle b = \angle d$

> $\angle a$ and $\angle c$ are vertically opposite angles.
>
> $\angle b$ and $\angle d$ are also vertically opposite angles.

> Vertically opposite angles are **equal**.

∠p, ∠q and ∠r are **angles on a straight line**.
Measure the unknown angles.

∠p = 50°

∠q = ☐ °

∠r = ☐ °

∠p + ∠q + ∠r = ☐ °

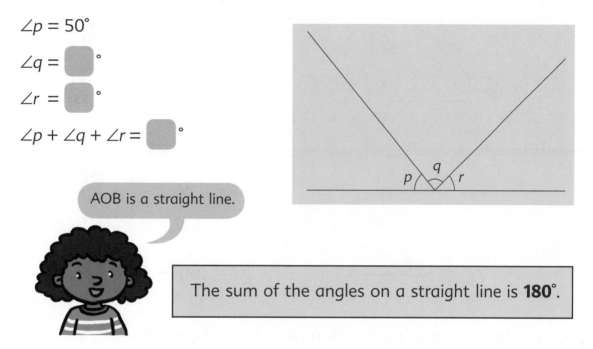

AOB is a straight line.

The sum of the angles on a straight line is **180°**.

∠x, ∠y and ∠z are **angles at a point**.
Measure the unknown angles.

∠x = 60°

∠y = ☐ °

∠z = ☐ °

∠x + ∠y + ∠z = ☐ °

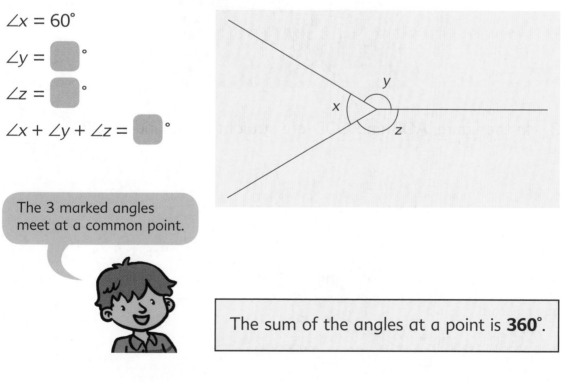

The 3 marked angles meet at a common point.

The sum of the angles at a point is **360°**.

1. Find the unknown marked angle in each of the following:

    (a)

    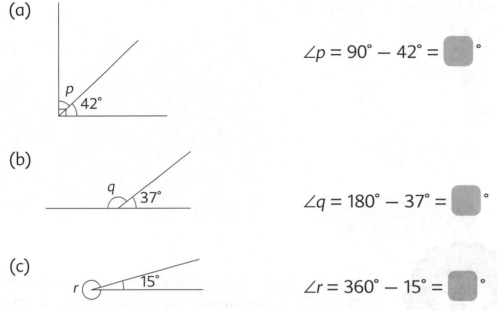

    $\angle p = 90° - 42° = \boxed{}°$

    (b)

    $\angle q = 180° - 37° = \boxed{}°$

    (c)

    $\angle r = 360° - 15° = \boxed{}°$

2. The figure shows 4 angles formed by two straight lines.
    If $\angle w = 46°$, find $\angle x$, $\angle y$ and $\angle z$.

    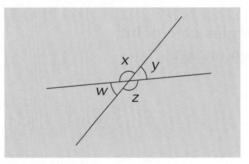

3. In the figure, AOB and COD are straight lines. Find $\angle COB$.

    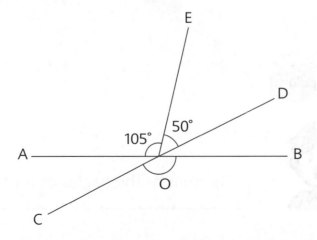

4. In the figure, ABC is a straight line.
   ∠ABD = 35° and ∠EBC = 55°. Find ∠DBE.

∠DBE = 180° − 35° − 55°

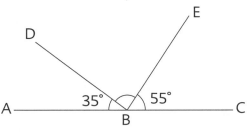

5. In the figure, find ∠x.

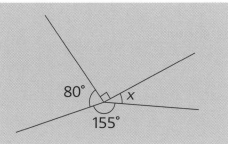

∠x = 360° − 90° − 80° − 155°

6. In the figure, find ∠m and ∠n.

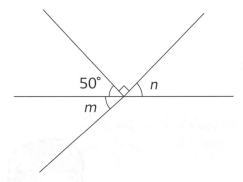

∠m and ∠n are vertically opposite angles.

7. Find the unknown marked angles.

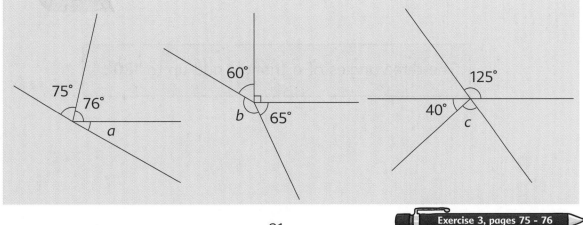

Exercise 3, pages 75 - 76

3 Sum of Angles of a Triangle

Trace and cut out this triangle.

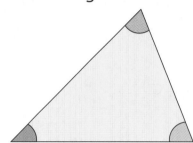

Then cut the triangle into 3 pieces as shown.

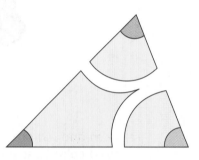

What do you notice when you arrange the 3 pieces like this?

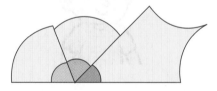

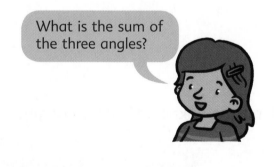

What is the sum of the three angles?

The three angles of a triangle add up to **180°**.

1. Measure and add up the angles in each triangle.

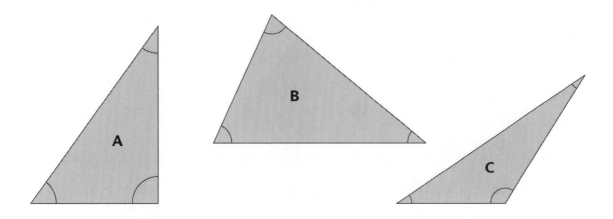

2. In Triangle ABC, ∠ABC = 82° and ∠BAC = 54°. Find ∠BCA.

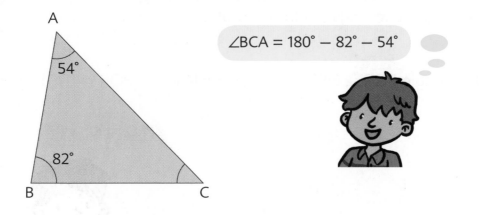

∠BCA = 180° − 82° − 54°

3. Find the unknown marked angle in each triangle.

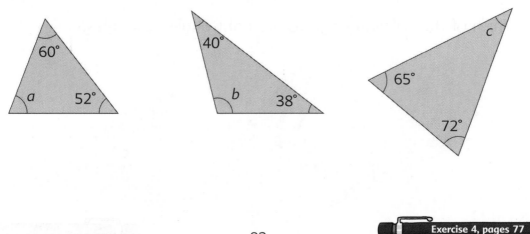

Exercise 4, pages 77

4. Fold a right-angled triangle like this:

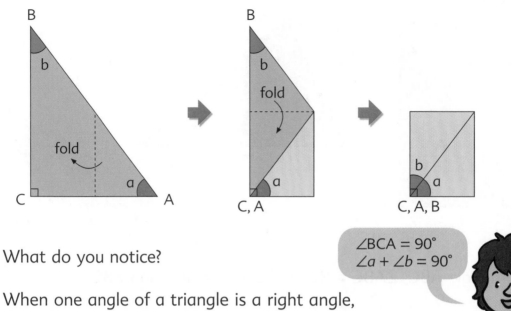

What do you notice?

∠BCA = 90°
∠a + ∠b = 90°

When one angle of a triangle is a right angle,
the other two angles add up to 90°.

5. In triangle PQR, ∠QPR is a right angle and ∠PQR = 57° Find ∠PRQ.

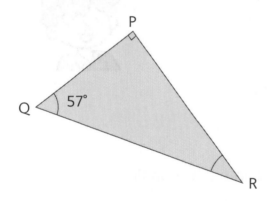

∠PRQ = 90° − 57°

6. Which of the following figures are right-angled triangles?

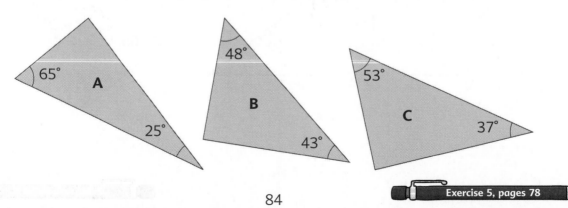

Exercise 5, pages 78

7. In triangle ABC, BC is extended to D.

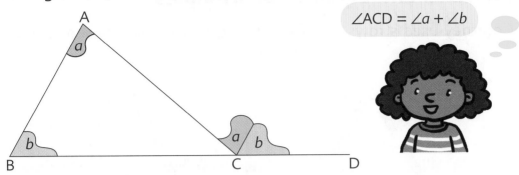

∠ACD is an **exterior angle** of the triangle.
∠a and ∠b are **interior opposite angles** of ∠ACD.

> The **exterior angle** of a triangle is equal to the sum of its **interior opposite angles**.

8. In triangle XYZ, YZ is extended to P, ∠ZXY = 50° and ∠XYZ = 34°. Find ∠XZP.

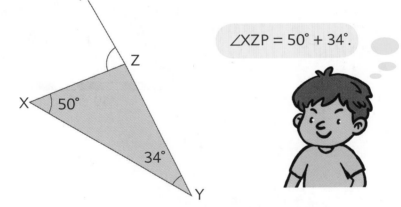

∠XZP = 50° + 34°.

9. In each figure, ACD is a straight line. Find the unknown marked angle.

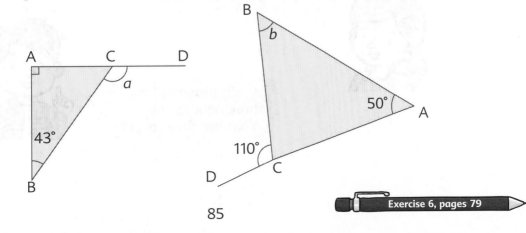

Exercise 6, pages 79

4 Isosceles and Equilateral Triangles

Courtney used straws of different lengths to make these triangles.

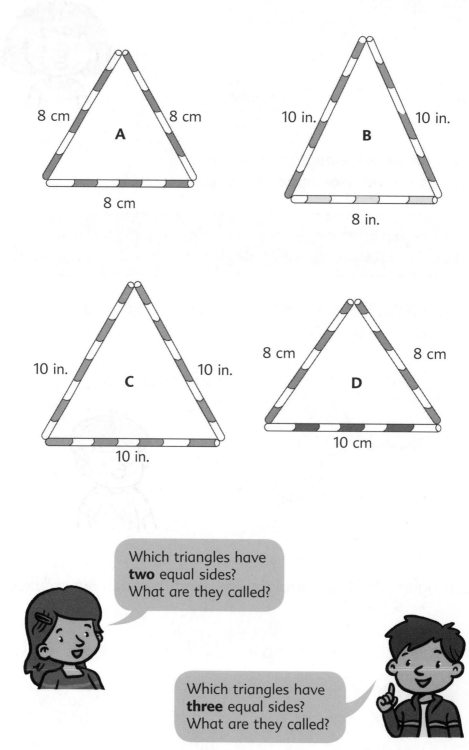

Which triangles have **two** equal sides?
What are they called?

Which triangles have **three** equal sides?
What are they called?

1. Fold an **isosceles triangle** in half as shown. What do you notice?

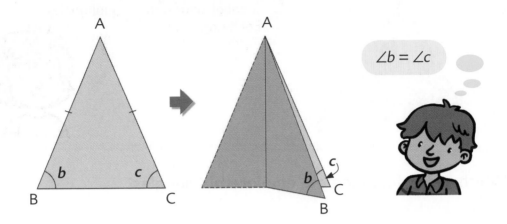

The angles opposite the equal sides are equal.

2. In triangle XYZ, ∠YXZ = ∠YZX. Is the triangle an isosceles triangle?

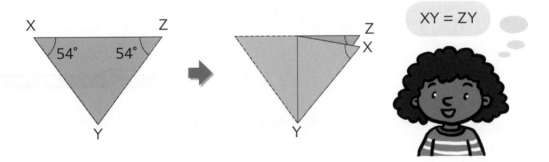

XYZ is an isosceles triangle.

3. Which of the following are isosceles triangles?

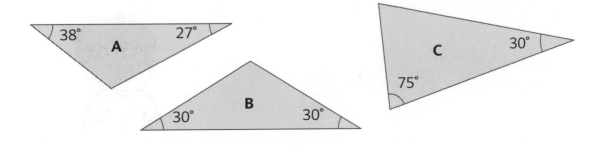

4.

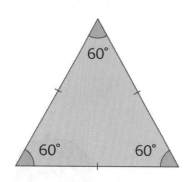

An **equilateral triangle** has 3 equal sides and 3 equal angles. Each angle is 60°.

Which of the following are **equilateral triangles**?

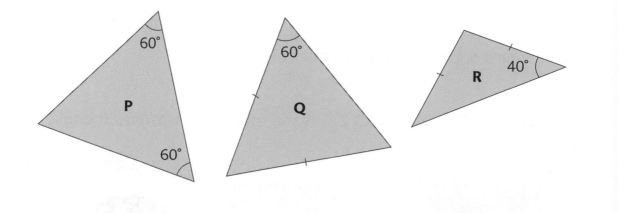

Exercise 7, pages 80 - 81

5. In triangle ABC, AB = AC and ∠ABC = 35°. Find ∠ACB and ∠BAC.

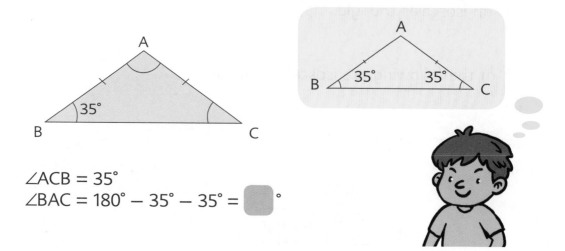

∠ACB = 35°
∠BAC = 180° − 35° − 35° = ⬜ °

88

6. In triangle PQR, QR = PR and ∠PQR = 65°. QRS is a straight line. Find ∠PRS.

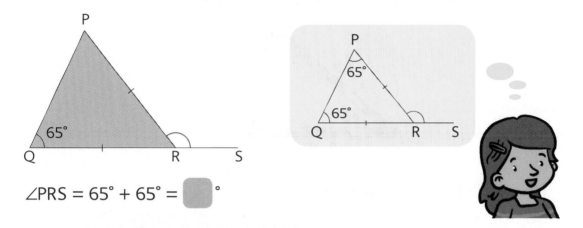

∠PRS = 65° + 65° = ⬜ °

7. In the figure, AB = AC and ∠DCE = 75°. BCD and ACE are straight lines. Find ∠ABC.

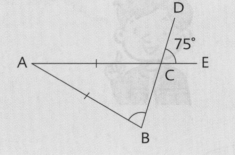

8. BCD is a straight line in each figure. Find the unknown marked angles.

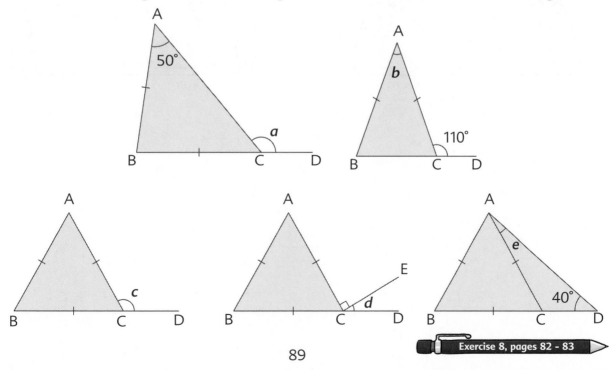

Exercise 8, pages 82 - 83

5 Drawing Triangles

Ali uses straws to make a triangle like this:

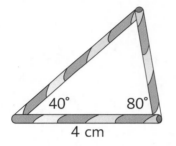

Then he draws the triangle.

> First, I draw the side 4 cm long. Then, I draw the two angles using a protractor.

1. Draw a triangle PQR in which PQ = 5 cm, ∠PQR = 90° and ∠QPR = 40°.

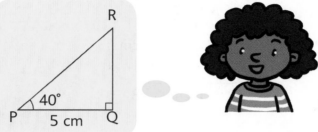

Step 1 Draw PQ = 5 cm.
Draw a line perpendicular to PQ through Q.

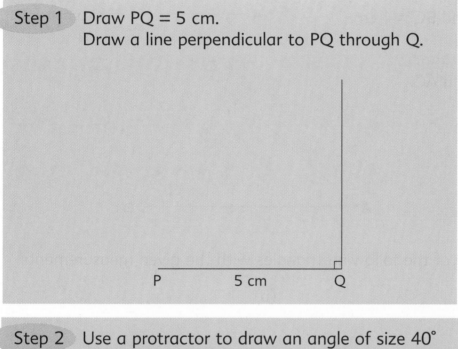

Step 2 Use a protractor to draw an angle of size 40° at P to locate the point R.

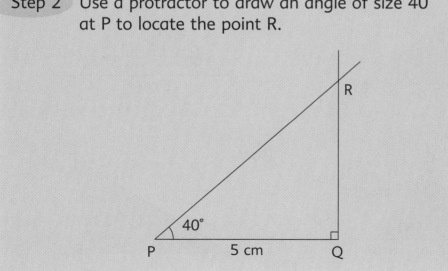

2. Draw a triangle ABC in which AB = 6 cm, BC = 4 cm and ∠ABC = 60°.

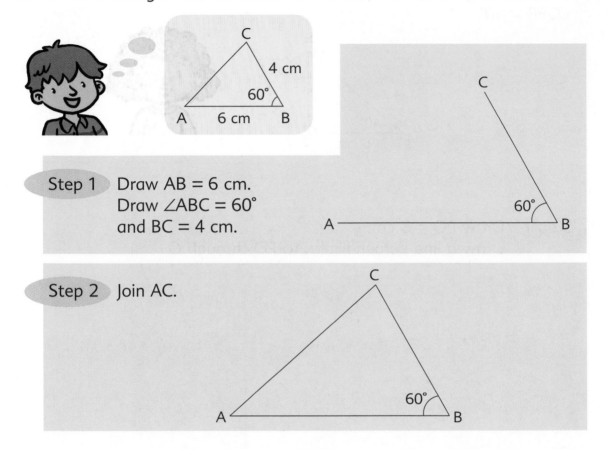

Step 1 Draw AB = 6 cm.
Draw ∠ABC = 60°
and BC = 4 cm.

Step 2 Join AC.

3. Draw each of the following triangles with the given measurements.

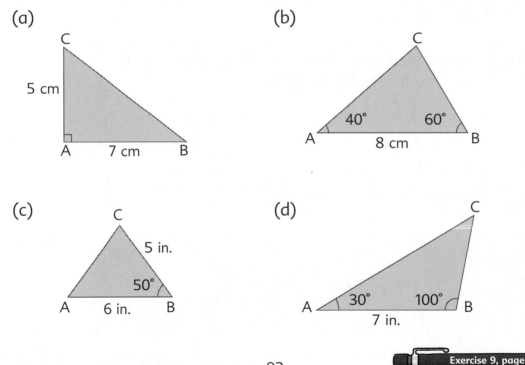

(a)

(b)

(c)

(d)

Exercise 9, page 84

6 Sum of Angles of a Quadrilateral

Draw a quadrilateral. Color each angle in a different color.

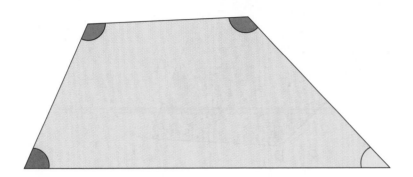

Then, tear off the angles.

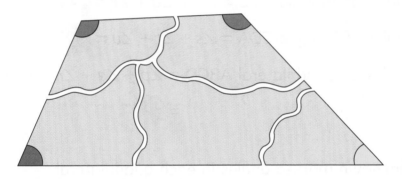

Place the angles together at a point.

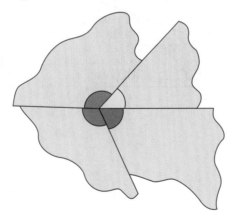

What do you notice?

> The angles of a quadrilateral add up to **360°**.

1.

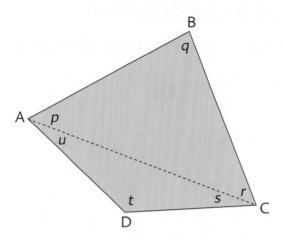

Sum of angles of Triangle ABC = ∠p + ∠q + ∠r = ⬜°

Sum of angles of Triangle CDA = ∠s + ∠t + ∠u = ⬜°

Sum of angles of Quadrilateral ABCD = ∠p + ∠q + ∠r + ∠s + ∠t + ∠u

= ⬜°

2. Find the unknown marked angles in each quadrilateral.

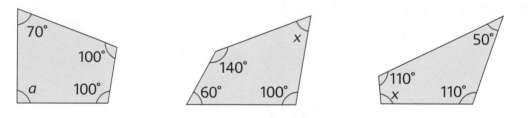

Exercise 10, page 85

7 Parallelograms, Rhombuses and Trapezoids

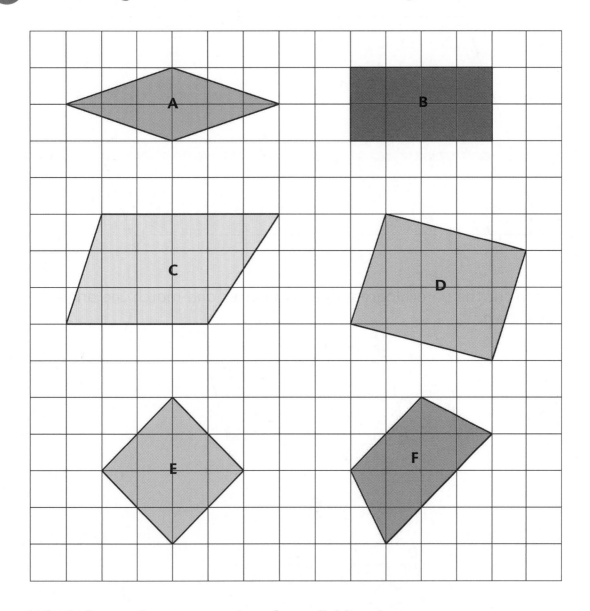

Which figures have two pairs of parallel lines?

Which figures have only one pair of parallel lines?

Which figures have four equal sides?

Which figures have four right angles?

What is the name of each figure?

1. Trace and cut out this parallelogram.

Then cut the parallelogram into two pieces and match the angles as shown.

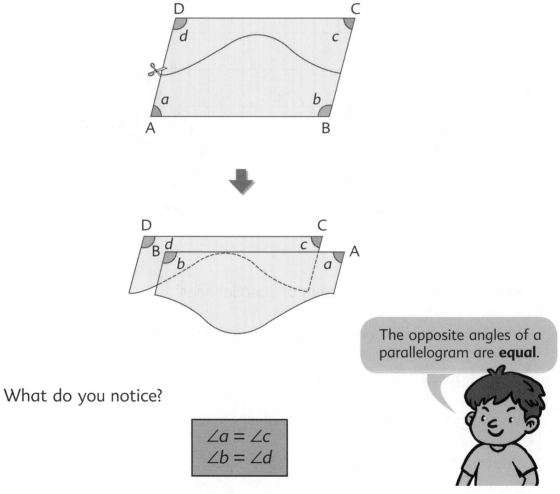

What do you notice?

$$\angle a = \angle c$$
$$\angle b = \angle d$$

The opposite angles of a parallelogram are **equal**.

2. (a)

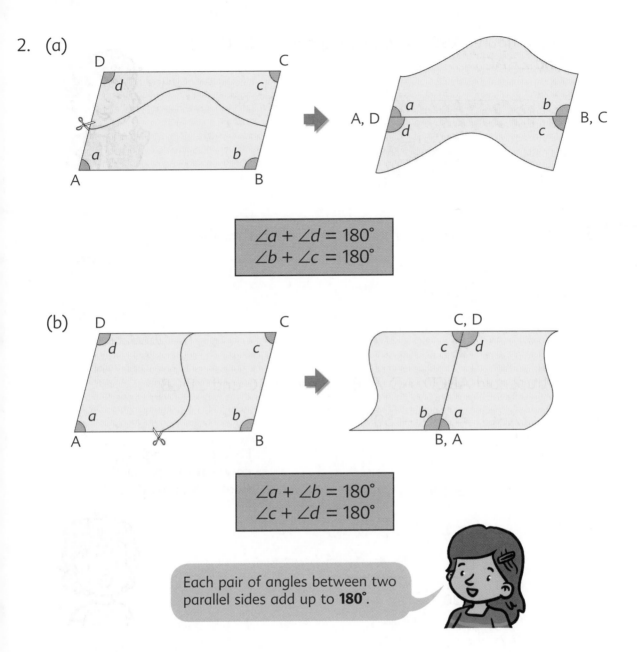

$$\angle a + \angle d = 180°$$
$$\angle b + \angle c = 180°$$

(b)

$$\angle a + \angle b = 180°$$
$$\angle c + \angle d = 180°$$

Each pair of angles between two parallel sides add up to **180°**.

3. Find the unknown marked angle in each parallelogram.

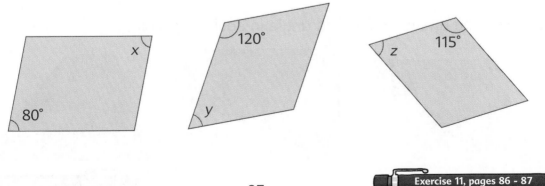

Exercise 11, pages 86 - 87

4. In the figure, ABCD is a rectangle and ∠DAC = 26°.
   Find ∠BAC.

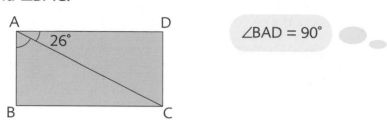

   ∠BAD = 90°

5. Find the unknown marked angle in each rhombus.

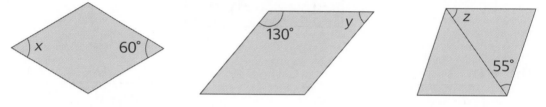

6. In trapezoid ABCD, AD // BC. Find ∠ABC and ∠DCB.

   ∠ABC = 180° − 50°

        = ◻ °

   ∠DCB = 180° − 120°

        = ◻ °

   Each pair of angles
   between two parallel
   sides add up to 180°.

7. Find the unknown marked angle in each trapezoid.

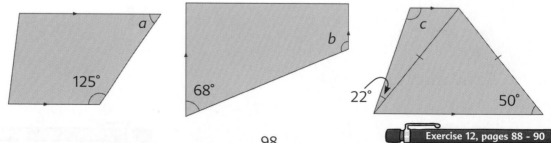

Exercise 12, pages 88 - 90

⑧ Drawing Parallelograms and Rhombuses

Weiming draws a pair of parallel lines.

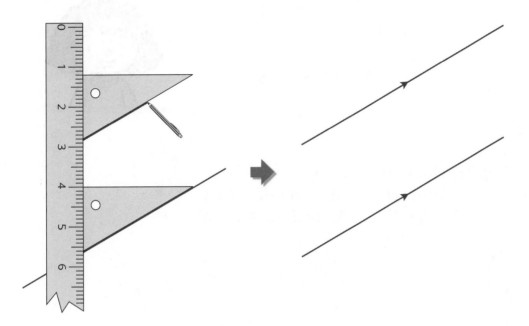

Then he draws another pair of parallel lines.

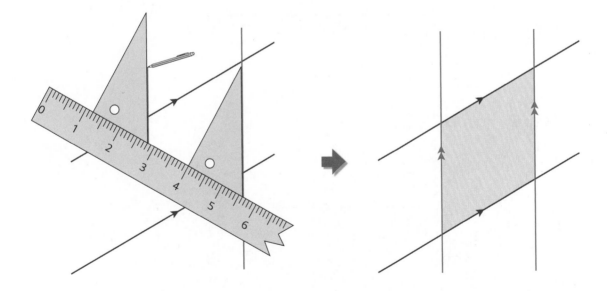

The shaded part of the figure is a parallelogram.

1. Draw a rectangle ABCD in which AB = 6 cm and AD = 3 cm.

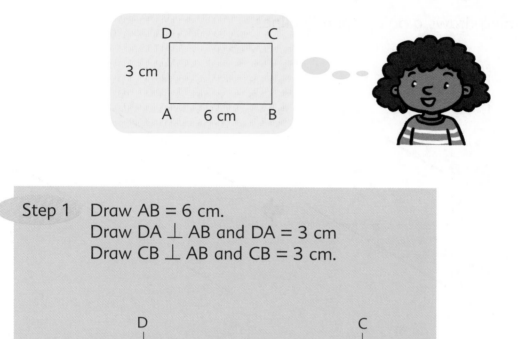

Step 1   Draw AB = 6 cm.
          Draw DA ⊥ AB and DA = 3 cm
          Draw CB ⊥ AB and CB = 3 cm.

Step 2   Join DC.

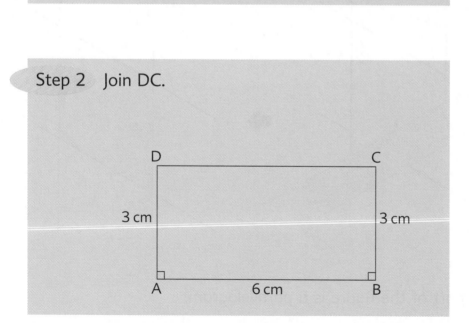

2. Draw a parallelogram ABCD in which AB = 4 cm, AD = 3 cm and ∠DAB = 60°.

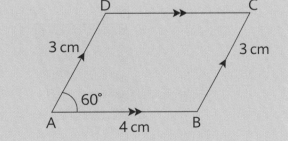

Step 1 Draw AB = 4 cm.
Draw ∠DAB = 60°
and AD = 3 cm.

Step 2 Draw BC // AD
and BC = 3 cm.

Step 3 Join DC.

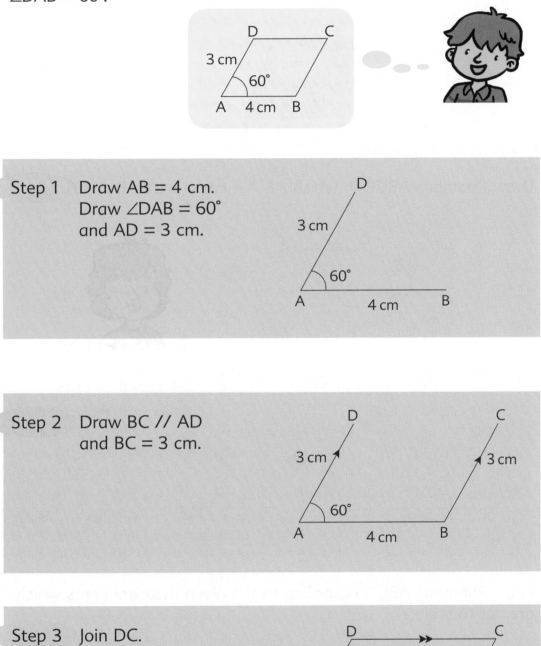

3. Draw Parallelogram PQRS according to the given measurements which are not to scale.

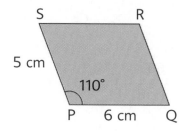

4. Draw Rhombus ABCD in which AB = 4 cm and ∠DAB = 40°.

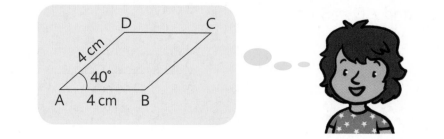

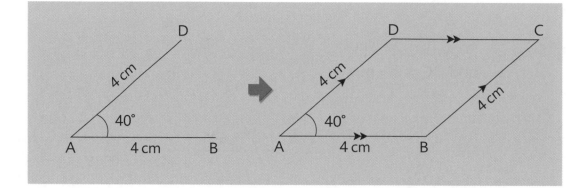

5. Draw Rhombus ABCD according to the given measurements which are not to scale.

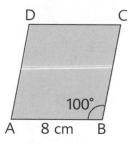

Exercise 13, pages 91 - 92

REVIEW 10

1. Find the value of each of the following:
   (a) 16 + 3 × 8 ÷ 4   (b) 30 + 85 × 2 ÷ (8 + 9)
   (c) (220 ÷ 11) × (28 − 5)   (d) 12 + (30 − 14) ÷ 4 × 5

2. Find the answer, rounded to the nearest whole number.
   (a) 2.56 × 32   (b) 45.62 × 0.6   (c) 56.32 ÷ 3.2

3. $\frac{2}{3}$ of a box of paper clips are red and the rest are green. If there are 120 red paper clips, how many green paper clips are there?

4. Mr. Reed packed $\frac{3}{4}$ kg of cookies equally into 3 bags. Find the weight of each bag of cookies. Give the answer in kilograms.

5. Mr. Lee's monthly salary is $2500. He gives $\frac{1}{5}$ of it to his wife and spends $\frac{3}{4}$ of the remainder. How much money does he spend each month?

6. The lengths of 3 rods are in the ratio 1 : 3 : 4. If the total length is 96 cm, find the length of the longest rod.

7. Carlos has $2.50. Tom has twice as much as Carlos. Ryan has $5 more than Tom. How much do the three boys have altogether?

8. After cutting off a length of 6.32 m from a rope 20 m long, the remainder is divided into 8 equal pieces. What is the length of each piece? Give the answer in meters.

9. What percentage of each figure is shaded?
   (a)   (b)

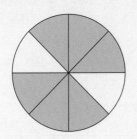
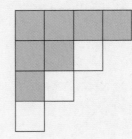

10. Express 80% as a decimal.

11. Express 36% as a fraction in its simplest form.

12. Express each of the following as a percentage.
    (a) 0.9   (b) 0.08   (c) $\frac{29}{50}$ (d) $\frac{27}{300}$

13. Find the value of each of the following:
    (a) 7% of 160   (b) 80% of 98 kg   (c) 15% of $21

14. 150 students took a Mathematics test. 98% of them passed the test. How many students passed the test?

15. Brandy made 250 donuts. She sold 90% of them. How many donuts did she have left?

16. Lynn deposits $5000 in a bank which pays 4% interest per year. How much money will she have in the bank after 1 year?

17. The usual price of a pair of shoes was $45. It was sold at a discount of 20%. Find the selling price.

18. Find the area of each shaded part.
    (a)   (b)

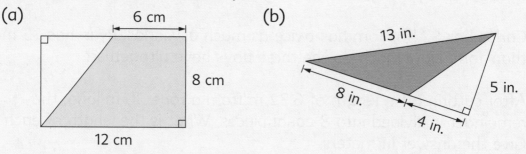

19. In each of the following figures, not drawn to scale, find ∠x. AOB and COD are straight lines.
    (a)   240°   (b)

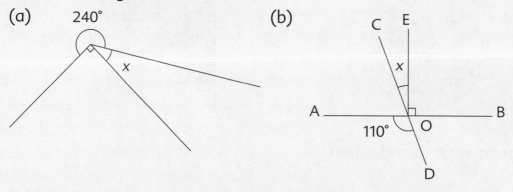

20. Estimate and then find the marked angles by measurement.

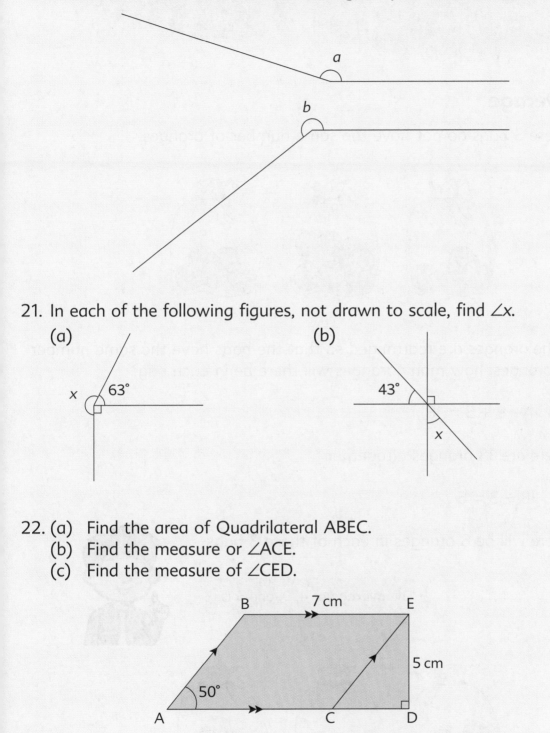

21. In each of the following figures, not drawn to scale, find ∠x.

(a)

x   63°

(b)

43°

x

22. (a) Find the area of Quadrilateral ABEC.
    (b) Find the measure or ∠ACE.
    (c) Find the measure of ∠CED.

B   7 cm   E

5 cm

50°

A   C   D

11 AVERAGE AND RATE

1 Average

These 3 bags do not have the same number of oranges.

If the oranges are rearranged so that the bags have the same number of oranges, how many oranges will there be in each bag?

$$4 + 9 + 5 = 18$$

There are 18 oranges altogether.

$$18 \div 3 = 6$$

There will be 6 oranges in each of these 3 bags.

The **average** of 4, 9, and 5 is 6.

1.

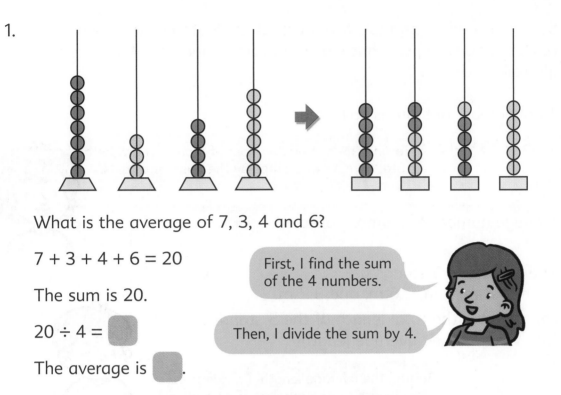

What is the average of 7, 3, 4 and 6?

$7 + 3 + 4 + 6 = 20$

The sum is 20.

First, I find the sum of the 4 numbers.

$20 \div 4 =$ ⬜

Then, I divide the sum by 4.

The average is ⬜.

2. This picture graph shows the number of fish caught by 3 boys. On the average, how many fish did each boy catch?

Andy	🐟🐟🐟🐟🐟
Christian	🐟🐟🐟🐟🐟🐟🐟
Jamal	🐟🐟🐟

$5 + 7 + 3 = 15$

The 3 boys caught 15 fish altogether.

$15 \div 3 =$ ⬜

On the average, each boy caught ⬜ fish.

3. Sally collected 36 stamps, Mary collected 38 stamps and Lilian collected 40 stamps. What was the average number of stamps each girl collected?

    Total number of stamps collected

    = 36 + 38 + 40

    = ⬚

    To find the average number of stamps, I divide the total number of stamps by the number of girls.

    Average number of stamps collected = ⬚

4. The lengths of 5 strings are
    1.4 m, 1.8 m, 2 m, 2.6 m, and 3.2 m.
    (a) What is the total length of the 5 strings?
    (b) What is their average length?

    To find the average length, I divide the total length by the number of strings.

5. The table shows the points Ron scored.
    (a) What is his total score for the 4 tests?
    (b) What is his average score?

Test A	68
Test B	76
Test C	78
Test D	88

6. A taxi driver traveled a total distance of 1659 km in 7 days. Find the average distance he traveled per day.

    1659 km ÷ 7

Exercise 1, pages 97 - 100

7. Jesse's average score for 5 tests is 74.6.
    Find his total score.

8. Warner spent an average of $4.65 per day for 8 days. How much did he spend altogether?

    $4.65 × 8

9. The average weight of 3 boxes is 1 kg 400 g. Find their total weight.

Total weight = 3 × 1 kg 400 g

   = ⬚ kg ⬚ g

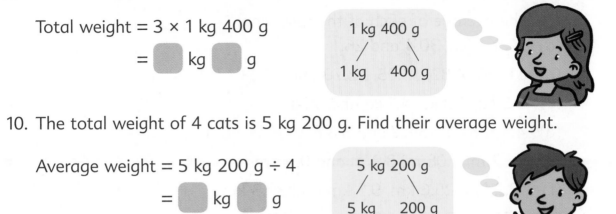

1 kg 400 g
／　　＼
1 kg　400 g

10. The total weight of 4 cats is 5 kg 200 g. Find their average weight.

Average weight = 5 kg 200 g ÷ 4

   = ⬚ kg ⬚ g

5 kg 200 g
／　　＼
5 kg　200 g

11. David took 15 minutes 20 seconds to cycle a distance of 2 km. On the average, how long did he take to cycle 1 km?

12. Peter took an average of 2 minutes 45 seconds to cycle 1 km. How long would he take to cycle 3 km?

Exercise 2, pages 101 – 102

13. The average height of two boys is 1.55 m. The height of one boy is 1.62 m. What is the height of the other boy?

   1.55 × 2 = 3.1

The total height of the two boys is 3.1 m.

   3.1 − 1.62 = ⬚

The height of the other boy is ⬚ m.

14. The average cost of 3 books is $4.50. The average cost of two of the books is $3.90. Find the cost of the third book.

   $4.50 × 3 = $13.50

The total cost of the 3 books is $13.50.

   $3.90 × 2 = $7.80

The total cost of two of the books is $7.80.

   $13.50 − $7.80 = $⬚

The cost of the third book is $⬚.

Exercise 3, page 103

PRACTICE A

1. Find the average of each of the following:
   (a) 12.5, 36.2, 30.4 and 26.1
   (b) $1.35, $4.82, $3.05, $2.70 and $2.13
   (c) 3.5 kg, 3.8 kg, 4.1 kg and 5 kg
   (d) 4.6 ℓ, 6.4 ℓ, 5.8 ℓ and 3.8 ℓ
   (e) 2.62 m, 2.08 m, 3.9 m and 0.96 m
   (f) 12.2 km, 25.6 km, 9.5 km and 30.3 km
   (g) 4.81 gal, 3.52 gal, 3.59 gal and 2 gal
   (h) 9.5 in., 7.25 in., 11.9 in., 4.11 in. and 6.09 in.

2. Rowley traveled 5460 km in 3 months. What was the average distance he traveled per month?

3. A man has 6 packages. Their average weight is 18 kg. Find the total weight of the 6 packages.

4. 4 people had lunch together. They spent an average of $3.75 each. What was the total cost of the lunch?

5. On the average, Violet spent 1 hour 20 minutes a day reading storybooks. How much time did she spend reading storybooks in 5 days?

6. Sam used 10 ℓ 275 ml of gas in 3 days. On the average, how much gas did he use per day?

7. The average cost of 2 storybooks was $2.45. One of the books cost $2.80. Find the cost of the other book.

8. An average of 145 people visited a 4-day exhibition in the first 3 days. Another 205 people visited the exhibition on the fourth day. What is the average number of visitors per day?

② Rate

A machine fills 60 similar bottles of syrup in 5 minutes. How many such bottles of syrup can it fill in one minute?

The machine fills the same number of bottles every minute.

In 5 minutes, the machine fills 60 bottles.
In 1 minute, it fills ___ bottles.

$$60 \div 5 = 12$$

The machine fills the bottles at the **rate** of 12 bottles per minute. It means the machine fills 12 bottles every minute.

1. Robert is paid $20 for working 4 hours. How much is he paid per hour?

$20 \div 4 = 5$

The rate is $5 per hour.

He is paid $5 per hour.

2. Water is flowing from a tap at the rate of 100 liters every 4 minutes. Find the rate of flow of water in liters per minute.

$100 \div 4 = $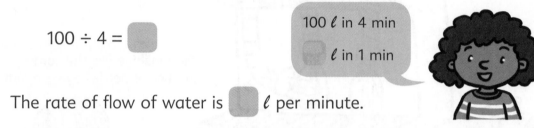

100 ℓ in 4 min

☐ ℓ in 1 min

The rate of flow of water is ☐ ℓ per minute.

3. A machine makes similar toy cars at the rate of 120 per minute. How many such toy cars will it make in 6 minutes?

$120 \times 6 = $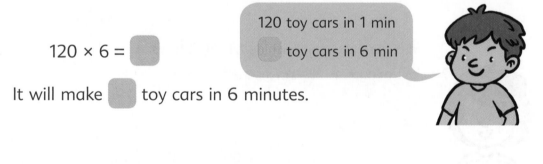

120 toy cars in 1 min

☐ toy cars in 6 min

It will make ☐ toy cars in 6 minutes.

4. A lamp can flash 5 times per minute. At this rate, how many times can it flash in 30 minutes?

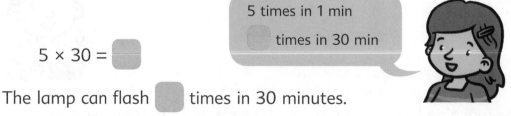

5 times in 1 min

☐ times in 30 min

$5 \times 30 = $ ☐

The lamp can flash ☐ times in 30 minutes.

Exercise 4, pages 104 - 105

5. Water is flowing from a tap at the rate of 25 gal per minute.

(a) How much water can be collected from the tap in 5 minutes?

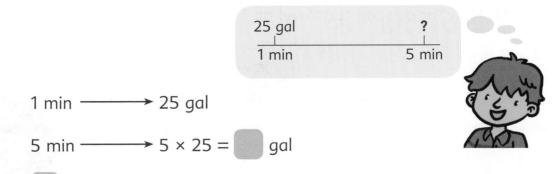

25 gal | 1 min   ? | 5 min

1 min ⟶ 25 gal

5 min ⟶ 5 × 25 = ☐ gal

☐ gal of water can be collected from the tap in 5 minutes.

(b) How long will it take to fill a container of capacity 100 gal?

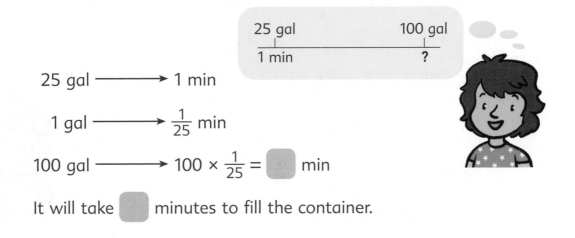

25 gal | 1 min   100 gal | ?

25 gal ⟶ 1 min

1 gal ⟶ $\frac{1}{25}$ min

100 gal ⟶ $100 \times \frac{1}{25}$ = ☐ min

It will take ☐ minutes to fill the container.

6. Mrs. Ricci types 45 words per minute. At this rate, how long will she take to type 135 words?

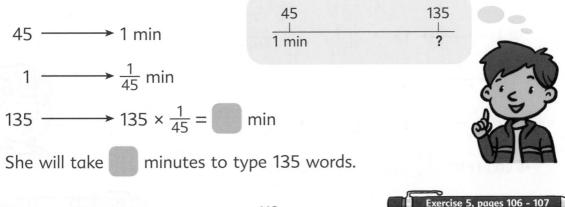

45 | 1 min   135 | ?

45 ⟶ 1 min

1 ⟶ $\frac{1}{45}$ min

135 ⟶ $135 \times \frac{1}{45}$ = ☐ min

She will take ☐ minutes to type 135 words.

Exercise 5, pages 106 - 107

7. A car can travel 96 km on 8 liters of gas.

The rate is 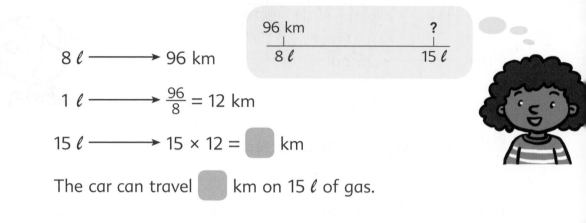 km per liter.

(a) How far can the car travel on 15 liters of gas?

8 ℓ ——→ 96 km

1 ℓ ——→ $\frac{96}{8}$ = 12 km

15 ℓ ——→ 15 × 12 = ⬜ km

The car can travel ⬜ km on 15 ℓ of gas.

(b) How much gas will be used if the car travels a distance of 120 km?

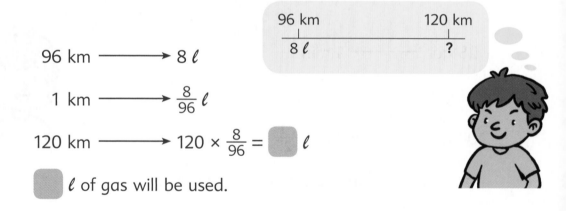

96 km ——→ 8 ℓ

1 km ——→ $\frac{8}{96}$ ℓ

120 km ——→ 120 × $\frac{8}{96}$ = ⬜ ℓ

⬜ ℓ of gas will be used.

8. A photocopier can print 12 copies in 48 seconds. At this rate, how many copies can it print in 1 minute?

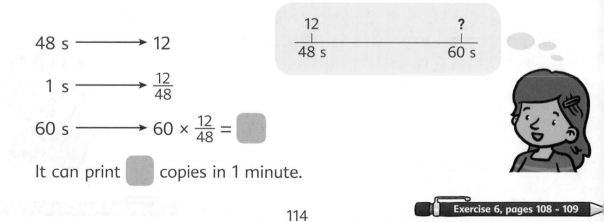

48 s ——→ 12

1 s ——→ $\frac{12}{48}$

60 s ——→ 60 × $\frac{12}{48}$ = ⬜

It can print ⬜ copies in 1 minute.

Exercise 6, pages 108 - 109

9. The table shows the rates of charges at a parking lot.

8:00 a.m. to 5:00 p.m.	$1 per $\frac{1}{2}$ hour
After 5:00 p.m.	$1 per hour

Mr. Karlson parked his car there from 1:30 p.m. to 7:00 p.m. How much did he have to pay?

> The duration from 1:30 p.m. to 5:00 p.m. is $3\frac{1}{2}$ h.

Parking fee from 1:30 p.m. to 5:00 p.m. = $7
Parking fee from 5:00 p.m. to 7:00 p.m. = $2

Total parking fee = $☐

Mr. Karlson had to pay $☐.

10. The workers in a factory are paid the following rates.

Weekdays	$28 per day
Saturdays and Sundays	$38 per day

Mr. Henderson worked from Friday to the following Tuesday. How much was he paid?

Mr. Henderson's pay for 3 weekdays

> Mr. Henderson worked for 5 days.

= $28 × 3 = $☐

Mr. Henderson's pay for Saturday and Sunday

= $38 × 2 = $☐

Total pay = $☐

Mr. Henderson was paid $☐.

11. The table shows the postage rates for sending magazines to another state.

Weight-step not over	Postage
20 g	$0.30
50 g	$0.40
100 g	$0.70
Per additional step of 100 g	$0.60

(a) Find the postage for a magazine which weighs 85 g.

Postage for 85 g = $ ☐

The postage is $ ☐ .

> 85 g is more than 50 g but less than 100 g.

(b) Find the postage for a magazine which weighs 330 g.

Postage for the 1st 100 g = $0.70

Postage for the next 230 g = $0.60 × 3 = $ ☐

Total postage = $ ☐

The postage is $ ☐ .

> 330 g is 230 g more than 100 g.

12. In a city, the rates of charges for taxi fare are as shown in the table:

Find the taxi fare for a trip of $5\frac{1}{2}$ km.

Fare for the 1st km = $2.40

Fare for the next $4\frac{1}{2}$ km = $0.40 × 5

= $ ☐

For the first km	$2.40
For every additional km	$0.40

Total fare = $ ☐

The taxi fare for a trip of $5\frac{1}{2}$ km is $ ☐ .

Exercise 7, pages 110 - 111

1. A machine can print 50 similar pages per minute. At this rate, how long will it take to print 2500 such pages?

2. A machine takes 4 minutes to seal 16 cookie boxes of the same kind. How many such cookie boxes can it seal in 1 minute?

3. Maggie's heart beats at the rate of 152 times every 2 minutes. At this rate, how many times does it beat in 30 minutes?

4. A pool is filled with water at the rate of 100 gal every 5 minutes. How long will it take to fill the pool with 1000 gal of water?

5. The cost of cementing 30 m² of floor area is $810. How much will it cost to cement 55 m² of floor area?

6. A wheel covers a distance of 40 m when it makes 25 revolutions. At this rate, what distance will it cover when it makes 50 revolutions?

7. The table shows the postage rates for local letter-delivery in Singapore. Find the postage for a letter which weighs

   (a) 55 g

   (b) 400 g

Weight-step not over	Postage
20 g	$0.25
40 g	$0.31
100 g	$0.50
250 g	$0.80
500 g	$1.00

8. The rental rates of a ski chalet are shown in the table.

   (a) Warner rented the chalet from Friday to Sunday. How much rent did he pay?

   (b) A group of friends rented 2 chalets from Wednesday to Saturday. How much did they pay altogether?

Weekdays	$60 per day
Saturdays and Sundays	$80 per day

1. (a) Express $2\frac{1}{4}$ kg in grams.

   (b) Express 3 km 90 m in kilometers.

   (c) Express $2\frac{3}{10}$ m in meters and centimeters.

2. A concert started at 7:15 p.m. and lasted $1\frac{2}{3}$ hours. At what time did it end?

3. $\frac{2}{5}$ of the people at a concert are children. $\frac{1}{4}$ of the children are boys. What fraction of the people at the concert are boys?

4. If 1 kg of beef costs \$12, find the cost of $\frac{3}{4}$ kg of beef.

5. $\frac{5}{8}$ of a sum of money is \$240. What is the value of the sum of money?

6. The factors of 24 are 1, 2, 3, 4, 6, 8 ▢ and 24. What is the missing factor in the ▢?

7. Find the prime factorization of 50.

8. Find the average value of each following set of data.
   (a) 185, 103, 127, 165
   (b) 3.8 cm, 2.7 cm, 4.5 cm, 1.6 cm

9. The average of five numbers is 40. If four of the numbers are 18, 27, 37, and 50, what is the fifth number?

10. Express each ratio in its simplest form.
    (a) 2 : 10   (b) 6 : 12   (c) 21 : 14
    (d) 20 : 5   (e) 40 : 16   (f) 4 : 100

11. Find the missing number in each ▢.

    (a) 5 : 6 = ▢ : 18   (b) 30 : 48 = 5 : ▢

12. $\frac{2}{5}$ of the 40 students in a class are girls. $\frac{1}{4}$ of the girls wear glasses. How many girls do not wear glasses?

13. Jason had 14 boxes of apples for sale. There were 36 apples in each box. He sold $\frac{5}{6}$ of the apples and threw away $\frac{1}{6}$ of the remainder which were rotten. How many apples did he have left?

14. After spending $\frac{2}{5}$ of her money on a handbag and $20 on a belt, Mary had $25 left. How much money did she have at first?

15. $\frac{3}{5}$ of a group of children are boys. There are 12 more boys than girls. How many girls are there?

16. The ratio of the number of red buttons to the number of green buttons is 4 : 3. There are 20 red buttons.
    (a) How many green buttons are there?
    (b) How many buttons are there altogether?

17. Lily, Carla and Gwen shared $156 in the ratio 3 : 2 : 7.
    (a) How much money did Carla receive?
    (b) How much more money did Gwen receive than Lily?

18. Mrs. Washington made 500 cookies. She sold 96% of them. How many cookies did she sell?

19. Marisol had $350. She spent 35% of the money on a pressure cooker. How much money did she have left?

20. The usual price of a motorcycle was $3600. Eric bought the motorcycle at a discount of 15%. How much did he pay?

21. The cost of a TV set was $640. Patrick sold it at 10% above the cost price. Find the selling price.

22. The perimeter of a square is 36 cm. Find the area of the square.

24. A picture measuring 28 cm by 25 cm is mounted on a rectangular cardboard, leaving a margin of 5 cm all around. Find the area of the cardboard not covered by the picture.

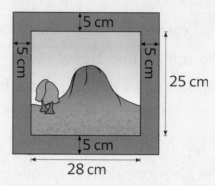

25. In the figure, ACE and BCD are straight lines. The figure is not drawn to scale. Find ∠x.

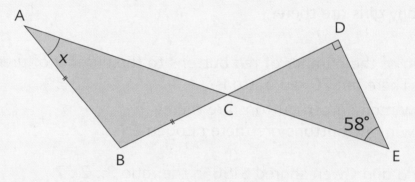

26. In Quadrilateral ABCD, ∠ABC = 95°, ∠BCD = 83°, and ∠CDA = 62°. What is the measure of angle ∠DAB?

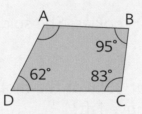

27. The area of a parallelogram is 53.3 cm². If the height is 6.5 cm, what is the length of the base?

28. What is the total surface area of a rectangular prism with a length of 14 in., a width of 4.5 in. and a height of 6.5 in.?

29. The area of the shaded face of the rectangular prism is 400 cm². Find the volume of the rectangular prism.

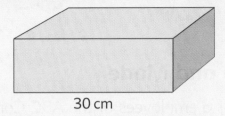

30 cm

30. The average weight of 3 packages is 2.2 kg. The average weight of two of them is 1.8 kg. Find the weight of the third package.

31. An empty rectangular tank measures 50 cm by 30 cm by 20 cm. It is to be filled with water from a tap.
    (a) How many liters of water are needed to fill up the tank?
    (b) If water flows from the tap at the rate of 12 liters per minute, how long will it take to fill up the tank? (1 liter = 1000 cm³)

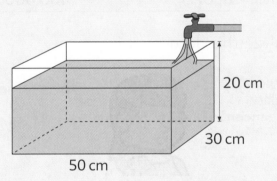

20 cm

30 cm

50 cm

32. A pool is filled with water at the rate of 20 liters per minute. How long will it take to fill the pool with 800 liters of water?

33. The table shows the postage rates for sending packages to Japan by air.

Find the postage for sending a package which weighs 800 g.

For first 250 g	$20.00
For every additional 250 g	$2.80

Review 11, pages 112 - 115

12 DATA ANALYSIS

1 Mean, Median and Mode

The yearly salaries of 6 employees of the ABC Company are listed below.

Employee	Salary
Mr. Chowdhury	$40,000
Miss Gallipoli	$40,000
Mrs. Workman	$40,000
Mr. Cruz	$50,000
Mrs. Menchon	$75,000
Mr. Capozzi	$100,000

How can we analyze this data?

I want to know the average salary, so I will find the **mean**.

The sum of all the values is $345,000.
$345,000 ÷ 6 = $57,500

I want to know what a middle level employee makes, so I will find the **median**.

There are 2 middle values, $40,000 and $50,000.
Find their average.
$40,000 + $50,000 = $90,000
$90,000 ÷ 2 = $45,000

I want to know what most people in the company make, so I will find the **mode**.

$40,000 is the value that appears the most often.

Mean, **median** and **mode** help us to look at data in different ways.

1. Timothy asked the students in the chess club their age. He recorded the information in a line plot.

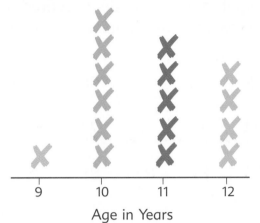

Age in Years

(a) What is the mean age of the people in the chess club?

(b) Make a list of the ages, in increasing order — 9, 10, 10, 10, ☐ ,
☐ , ☐ , ☐ , ☐ , ☐ , ☐ , ☐ , ☐ , ☐ , ☐ .

(c) What is the median age of the people in the chess club?

(d) How old are most of the people in the chess club?

Remember? With a line plot, we can also find the median by marking pairs of X's starting at the ends from the bottom up.

2. Danny recorded the high and low temperatures for 10 consecutive days in degrees Fahrenheit and recorded the data in a table.

	Day 1	Day 2	Day 3	Day 4	Day 5	Day 6	Day 7	Day 8	Day 9	Day 10
High Temp (°F)	73°	74°	75°	74°	79°	82°	81°	85°	83°	86°
Low Temp (°F)	62°	64°	62°	63°	65°	68°	66°	70°	69°	70°

(a) What was the average high temperature over the 10-day period?

(b) What was the average low temperature?

(c) List the high temperatures in order. What was the median high temperature?

(d) What was the median low temperature?

If there are 2 numbers in the middle that are different, then the number that is halfway between them is the median.

123

Exercise 1, pages 116 - 117

2 Histograms

The number of points that 24 students scored for a mathematics exam is shown below. How can we organize this data?

79	65	73	85	90	75	92	88
93	84	70	68	72	85	89	71
98	75	82	87	88	78	81	83

There are a lot of numbers but some are close to each other so I will group them.

Points	Number of Students
90 to 99	4
80 to 89	10
70 to 79	8
60 to 69	2

The data is grouped into four intervals.

The data in the table can be shown on a **histogram**.

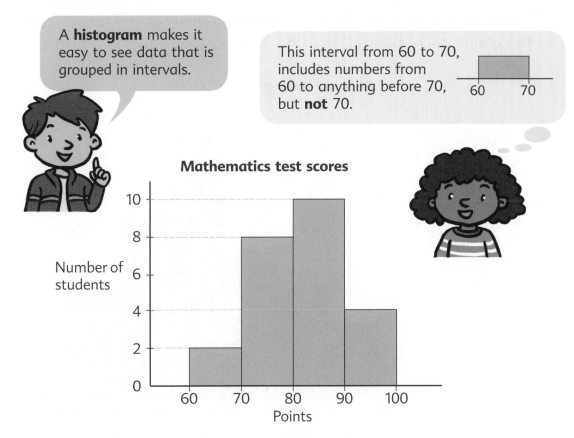

A **histogram** makes it easy to see data that is grouped in intervals.

This interval from 60 to 70, includes numbers from 60 to anything before 70, but **not** 70.

(a) What is the total number of students represented in the histogram?

(b) How many points are there in each interval?

(c) How many students scored at least 70 but fewer than 80 points?

(d) In which interval did most of the students score?

(e) In which interval did the fewest students score?

(f) Which interval represents the mode of the data?

(g) What percentage of students scored at least 90 but fewer than 100 points?

(h) What fraction of students scored at least 60 but fewer than 70 points?

(i) How many students scored in the 70 to 80 point interval?

125

1. Sarah did a survey to find out how many minutes her friends talk on the phone each month. Then she showed the results in a histogram.

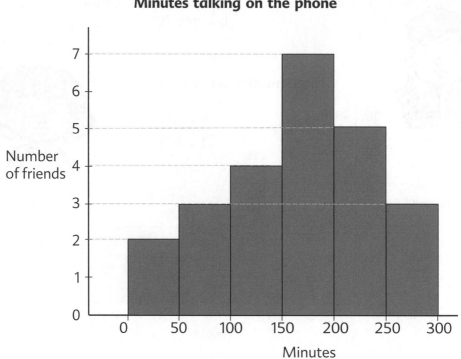

Minutes talking on the phone

(a) How many friends did Sarah survey?

(b) How many minutes are there in each interval of the histogram?

(c) Which interval shows the number of minutes most of her friends talked?

(d) How many friends talked at least 50 minutes but less than 200 minutes?

(e) What percentage of her friends talked at least 200 minutes but less than 300 minutes?

2. The histogram below shows the height of 5th grade students at Red Hill School.

Height of 5th grade students

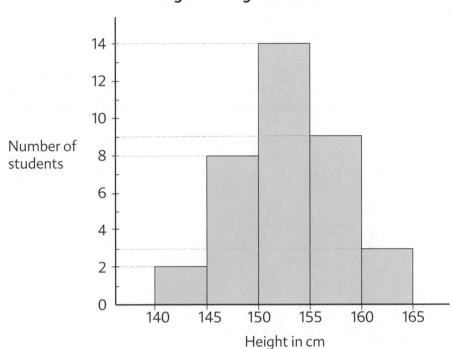

(a) What is the total number of students represented in the histogram?

(b) What is the height in cm represented in each interval?

(c) How many students are at least 145 cm tall but shorter than 150 cm?

(d) Which interval represents the mode height of the students?

(e) What percentage of the students are at least 155 cm tall but shorter than 160 cm?

(f) What fraction of the students are at least 155 cm tall but shorter than 165 cm?

Exercise 2, pages 118 - 121

3 Line Graphs

Danny created a line graph for the data he collected for the high and low temperatures over a 10-day period.

	Day 1	Day 2	Day 3	Day 4	Day 5	Day 6	Day 7	Day 8	Day 9	Day 10
High Temp (°F)	73°	74°	75°	74°	79°	82°	81°	85°	83°	86°
Low Temp (°F)	62°	64°	62°	63°	65°	68°	66°	70°	69°	70°

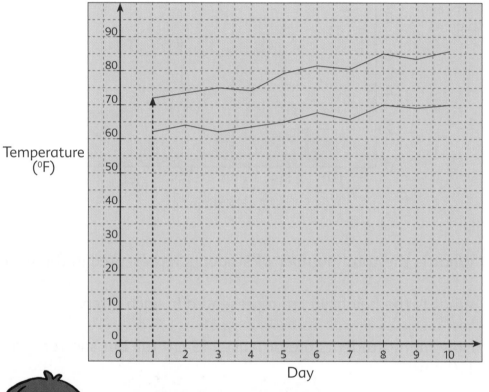

The point for the high temperature for the first day is at 73 on Day 1.

We can use a line graph to see if data changes over time.

(a) What values are on the horizontal axis?

(b) What values are on the vertical axis?

(c) How does the data change over time?

1. This line graph shows the height in inches for a boy from the age of 5 years to 11 years.

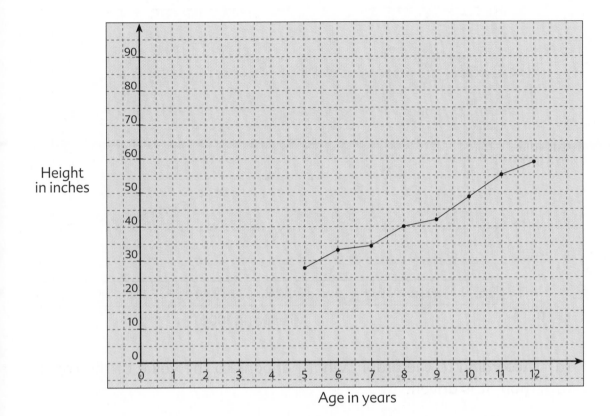

Height in inches

Age in years

(a) What can we say about the change in the boy's height over the years?

(b) What was his height when he was 8 years old?

(c) How old was he when he was 35 in. tall?

(d) Between which ages did the greatest increase in height take place?

2. This graph shows the average value of a car versus its mileage.

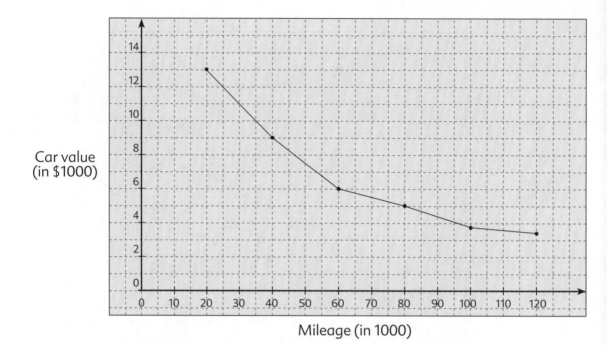

Car value
(in $1000)

Mileage (in 1000)

(a) According to the graph, what happens to the value of the car the more it is driven?

(b) About how much could the owner sell the car for if the mileage on the car is 70,000?

(c) The car is being sold for $10,000. The mileage is 50,000. Is this a good deal for the person buying the car?

130

Exercise 3, page 122

4 Pie Charts

The table shows the number of T-shirts of different sizes sold in a shop on a certain day.

Size	S	M	L	XL
Number of T-shirts	9	18	6	3

There are 36 T-shirts altogether.

$\frac{1}{4}$ of the T-shirts are of size S.

What fraction of the T-shirts are of size M?
What fraction of the T-shirts are of size L?
What fraction of the T-shirts are of size XL?

$\frac{9}{36} = \frac{1}{4}$

The fractions can be shown like this:

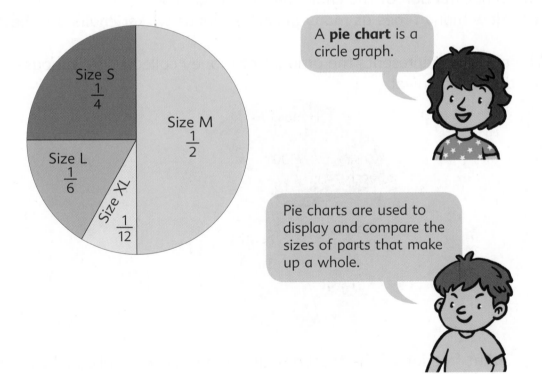

A **pie chart** is a circle graph.

Pie charts are used to display and compare the sizes of parts that make up a whole.

This is a **pie chart.** It represents the number of T-shirts of different sizes sold in the shop.

1. There are 200 chairs in a warehouse. 80 of them are plastic chairs, 30 are metal chairs, 40 are wicker chairs and the rest are wooden chairs. The pie chart represents the number of chairs of each type.

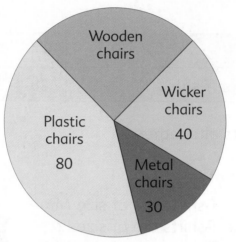

(a) Which type of chair is found in the greatest quantity?
(b) How many wooden chairs are there?
(c) What fraction of the chairs are plastic chairs?
(d) How many times as many plastic chairs as wicker chairs are there?

2. The pie chart represents the amount of money collected by various booths at a carnival.

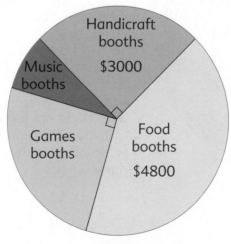

(a) What fraction of the total amount of money was collected by the games booths?
(b) What was the total amount of money collected by various booths?
(c) How much money was collected by the music booths?
(d) What was the ratio of the money collected by the food booths to the money collected by the handicraft booths?

Exercise 4, pages 123 - 126

3. A group of 40 boys were asked to choose toast, cereal, pancake or eggs for breakfast on a certain day. The pie chart represents their choices.

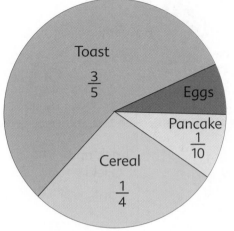

(a) Which type of breakfast did most students have on that day?
(b) What fraction of the students had eggs for breakfast?
(c) How many students had toast for breakfast?
(d) What percentage of the students had cereal for breakfast?

4. The students in a school were asked to name their favorite subject. The pie chart represents their choices.

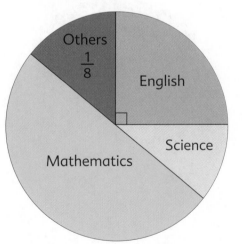

(a) What fraction of the students liked Mathematics?
(b) What percentage of the students liked English?
(c) What fraction of the students liked Science?
(d) If 1200 students liked Mathematics, how many students liked English?

Exercise 5, pages 127 - 129

5. A group of 200 students were asked to name their favorite sport. The pie chart represents their choices.

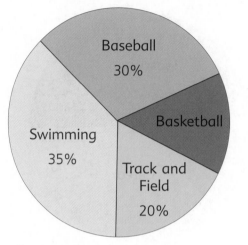

(a) Which was the most popular sport?
(b) What percentage of the students chose basketball?
(c) How many students chose baseball?
(d) What fraction of the students chose swimming?

6. Mrs. Gray spent some money on clothes. The pie chart shows how the money was spent.

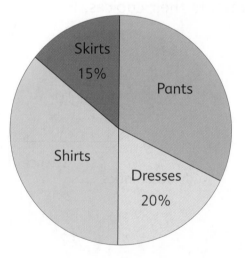

(a) What did Mrs. Gray spend the most amount of money on?
(b) What percentage of the money was spent on shirts?
(c) What percentage of the money was spent on pants?

Exercise 6, pages 130 - 133

1. Find the value of each of the following:
   (a) $60 \div (14 - 4) \times 3$ (b) $50 - 8 \times 2 + 16 \div 8$

2. Find the value of each of the following.
   (a) $4 - 1\frac{2}{3}$ (b) $72 \times \frac{7}{8}$
   (c) $\frac{3}{10} \times \frac{5}{6}$ (d) $\frac{8}{9} \div 6$

3. Write each of the following as a decimal.
   (a) $\frac{9}{100} + 3 + \frac{7}{10}$ (b) $\frac{37}{1000} + \frac{13}{100} + \frac{7}{10}$

4. Express 2.045 as a mixed number in its simplest form.

5. (a) Round 3.952 to 1 decimal place.
   (b) Round 7.639 to 2 decimal places.

6. An airplane traveled a distance of 2946 km. Round the distance to the nearest 1000 km.

7. The average of 63, 74, ▢ and 85 is 82. What is the missing number in the ▢?

8. Express 20 : 12 : 56 in its simplest form.

9. (a) Express 20 out of 25 as a percentage.
   (b) Express 90 out of 200 as a percentage.

10. Express 48% as a fraction in its simplest form.

11. How many minutes are there in $2\frac{3}{5}$ hours?

12. A cake weighs 1.5 kg. Find the weight of $\frac{1}{2}$ the cake.

13. Kate bought 8 spoons and 5 plates for $16.40. Each plate cost $1.20 more than each spoon. How much does each spoon cost?

14. A farmer sold 200 chickens at $3.50 each. With the money he received from the sale, he bought 30 turkeys. Find the cost of 1 turkey correct to the nearest cent.

15. The average weight of 2 boys is 48 kg. If one boy is 6 kg heavier than the other, find the weight of the heavier boy.

16. Sean spent $\frac{3}{5}$ of his money on a present for his mother. He spent $\frac{3}{4}$ of the remainder on a present for his sister.

    (a) What fraction of his money did he spend on the present for his sister?
    (b) If he spent $450 altogether, how much money did he have left?

17. A typist can type at a rate of 50 words per minute. How long will the typist take to type 4 pages each containing 300 words?

18. The rates of charges for taxi fare in a city are shown in the table.

    Find the taxi fare for a journey of 4 km.

For the first 1.5 km	$2.40
For every additional 100 m	$0.10

19. The ratio of the number of men to the number of women in a club is 5 : 7. There are 12 more women than men. How many members are there altogether?

20. There are 1800 students in a school. 60% of them are boys. How many more boys than girls are there?

21. In each of the following figures, not drawn to scale, find ∠y.
    (a) BCD is a straight line.   (b) ABC and CDE are straight lines.

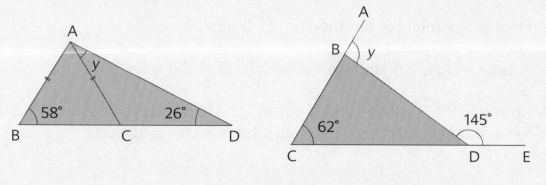

136

22. Find the area of the parallelogram.

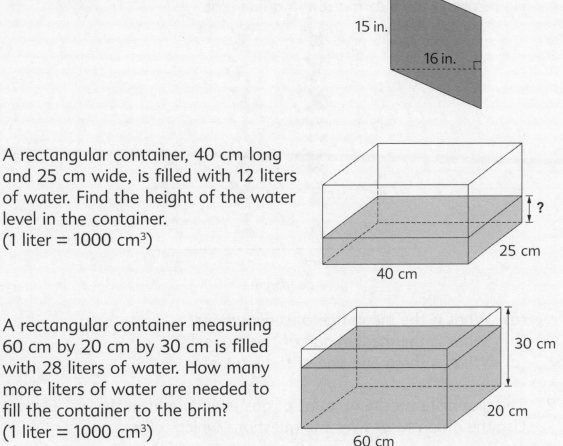

15 in.

16 in.

23. A rectangular container, 40 cm long and 25 cm wide, is filled with 12 liters of water. Find the height of the water level in the container.
(1 liter = 1000 cm³)

?

25 cm

40 cm

24. A rectangular container measuring 60 cm by 20 cm by 30 cm is filled with 28 liters of water. How many more liters of water are needed to fill the container to the brim?
(1 liter = 1000 cm³)

30 cm

20 cm

60 cm

25. A school has four classes in 5th grade. The table shows the number of boys and girls in each class.

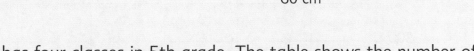

Class	Number of boys	Number of girls
A	23	15
B	18	20
C	17	19
D	20	18

(a) How many more boys than girls are there in 5th grade?
(b) What percentage of the students in 5th grade are boys?

26. Billy did a survey of the students in the drama club to find their ages. He recorded the information in a line plot.

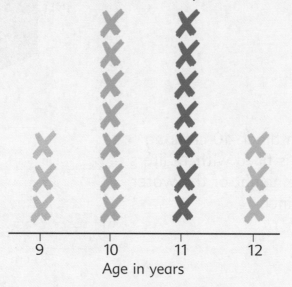

(a) What is the mean age of the students?
(b) What is the median age of the students?
(c) What is the mode age of the students?

27. The graph shows the amount of gas Jake bought in the last 6 months. Use the graph to answer the questions which follow.

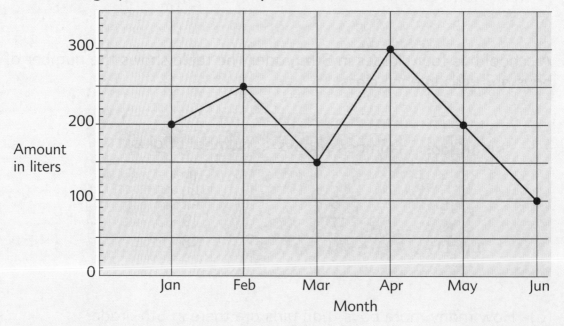

(a) Find the average amount of gas he bought each month.
(b) If 1 liter of gas cost $1.15, how much less money did he spend on gas in March than in February?

28. The bar graph shows the daily attendance of a class of 40 students.

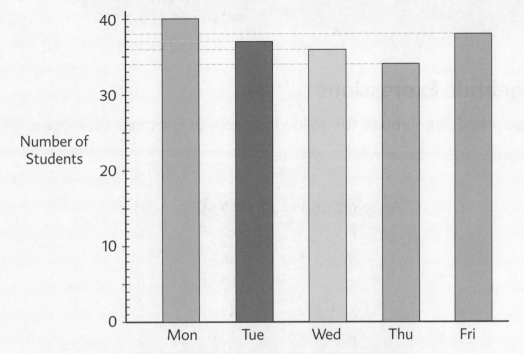

(a) On which day was the attendance the lowest?
(b) What percentage of the students were absent on Friday?
(c) What was the average daily attendance?

29. A group of students were asked to name their favorite activity in school. The pie chart represents their choices.

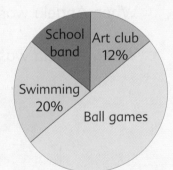

(a) What percentage of the students liked the school band?
(b) What fraction of the students liked swimming?
(c) If 18 students liked the art club, find the total number of students in the group.

30. A group of students were asked to choose an after-school activity they would like to join. The pie chart represents their choices.

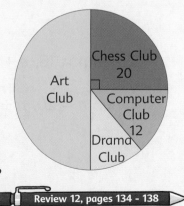

(a) How many students chose the Art Club?
(b) What percentage of the students chose the Chess Club?
(c) How many students chose the Drama Club?
(d) How many students were there in the group?

Review 12, pages 134 - 138

13 ALGEBRA

1 Algebraic Expressions

Angela and Limei made the following table to compare their ages.

Angela's age	Limei's age
6	8
7	9
8	10
9	11
10	12
⋮	⋮

When Angela was 12 years old, how old was Limei?

When Angela was 15 years old, how old was Limei?

Limei was 2 years older than Angela.

When Angela was n years old, Limei was $(n + 2)$ years old.

n stands for any whole number.

When $n = 16$, $n + 2 = 16 + 2 = 18$

When $n = 20$, $n + 2 = $

1. Alan is 8 years old.
   (a) How old will he be in 5 years' time?

   (b) How old will he be in *x* years' time?
       Give your answer in terms of *x*.

2. Jim has $2 more than Travis.
   (a) If Jim has $10, how much money does Travis have?

   (b) If Jim has $*m*, how much money does Travis have?
       Give your answer in terms of *m*.

3. Tracy bought *w* kg of flour. She used 5 kg of it.
   (a) Express the amount of flour left in terms of *w*.

   Amount of flour left = ($w - 5$) kg

   (b) If Tracy bought 8 kg of flour, how much flour did she have left?

   $w - 5 = 8 - 5 = $ ▢

   She had ▢ kg of flour left.

4. There are 4 apples in each packet.

(a) How many apples are there in *n* packets?

Number of packets	Total number of apples
1	4 × 1 = 4
2	4 × 2 = 8
3	4 × 3 = 12
4	4 × 4 = 16
5	4 × 5 = 20
n	4*n*

We write 4 × *n* as 4*n*.

(b) If *n* = 8, how many apples are there altogether?
(c) If *n* = 11, how many apples are there altogether?

5. There are 3 boxes of chicken wings. Each box contains *p* chicken wings.
   (a) Express the total number of chicken wings in terms of *p*.

   Total number of chicken wings = 3*p*

   3*p* means 3 × *p* or *p* × 3.

   (b) If each box contains 7 chicken wings,
       how many chicken wings are there altogether?

   3*p* = 3 × 7 = ▢

   There are ▢ chicken wings altogether.

6. A rectangular tile measures k cm by 8 cm. Express its area in terms of k.

$k \times 8 = 8k$

7. Ali has 8 boxes. He puts an equal number of marbles in each box.
   (a) If there is a total of 96 marbles, find the number of marbles in each box.

   Number of marbles in each box $= \frac{96}{8} =$ ▢

   (b) It there is a total of x marbles, find the number of marbles in each box in terms of x.

   Number of marbles in each box $= \frac{x}{8}$ We write $x \div 8$ as $\frac{x}{8}$.

8. Pearl buys 3 books.
   (a) If the total cost of the books is $12, find their average cost.

   Average cost $= \frac{\$12}{3} = \$$ ▢

   (b) If the total cost of the books is m, find their average cost in terms of m.

   Average cost $= \frac{\$m}{3} = \$\frac{m}{3}$ We write $m \div 3$ as $\frac{m}{3}$.

9. Find the value of each of the following when $n = 6$.
   (a) $n + 4$ (b) $10 + n$ (c) $15 - n$
   (d) $n - 6$ (e) $4n$ (f) $10n$
   (g) $\frac{n}{8}$ (h) $\frac{n}{6}$ (i) $\frac{n}{12}$

Exercise 1, pages 139 - 141

10. Tyrone has some marbles. He puts x marbles in a bag. There are 5 bags and 3 marbles altogether.
    (a) Express the total number of marbles in terms of x.

x marbles in each bag.
5x marbles in 5 bags.

    Total number of marbles = $5x + 3$

    (b) If $x = 10$, how many marbles does Tyrone have?

    $5x + 3 = 5 \times 10 + 3 = $ ☐

    Tyrone has ☐ marbles.

11. Find the value of $2x - 3$ when $x = 5$.
    $2x - 3 = 2 \times 5 - 3 = $ ☐

12. Jeff had $50. He gave $$y$ to his son. The remainder was then shared equally between his 2 daughters.
    (a) Express each daughter's share in terms of y.

    Amount of money shared by the 2 daughters = $\$(50 - y)$

    Amount of money each daughter received = $\$\dfrac{50 - y}{2}$

    (b) If $y = 12$, how much money did each daughter receive?
    $$\frac{50 - y}{2} = \frac{50 - 12}{2} = \boxed{}$$

    Each daughter received $\$$ ☐.

13. Find the value of $\dfrac{x - 4}{2}$ when $x = 12$.
    $$\frac{x - 4}{2} = \frac{12 - 4}{2}$$
    $$= \frac{8}{2}$$
    $$= \boxed{}$$

14. (a) Find the value of $\dfrac{4n + 3}{5}$ when $n = 8$.

$$\dfrac{4n + 3}{5} = \dfrac{4 \times 8 + 3}{5} = \boxed{}$$

(b) Find the value of $\dfrac{45 - 3r}{3}$ when $r = 5$.

$$\dfrac{45 - 3r}{3} = \dfrac{45 - 3 \times 5}{3} = \boxed{}$$

15. We write $y \times y = y^2$.

Find the value of the following when $y = 3$.

(a) y^2

$$y^2 = 3 \times 3 = \boxed{}$$

(b) $2y^2$

$$2y^2 = 2 \times 3 \times 3 = \boxed{}$$

(c) $\dfrac{y^2}{5}$

$$\dfrac{y^2}{5} = \dfrac{3 \times 3}{5} = \boxed{}$$

16. We write $a \times a \times a$ as a^3.

Find the value of the following when $a = 2$.

(a) a^3

$$a^3 = 2 \times 2 \times 2 = \boxed{}$$

(b) $a^3 + 1$

$$a^3 + 1 = 2 \times 2 \times 2 + 1 = \boxed{}$$

(c) $a^2 + a^3$

$$a^2 + a^3 = 2 \times 2 + 2 \times 2 \times 2 = \boxed{}$$

17. Find the value of each of the following when $a = 5$.

(a) $\dfrac{4a}{3}$ (b) $8 + 3a$ (c) $2a - 3$

(d) $\dfrac{a}{3} + 2$ (e) $\dfrac{3a - 4}{2}$ (f) $\dfrac{2a + 5}{5}$

(g) $2a^2 - 3$ (h) $a^3 + 5$ (i) $a^3 - a$

Exercise 2, pages 142 - 143

18. John has 4 bags of red beads and 3 bags of green beads. There are *x* beads in each bag.

(a) Find the total number of beads in terms of *x*.

Number of red beads $= 4x$

Number of green beads $= 3x$

Total number of beads $= 4x + 3x$

$= (4 + 3)x$

$= 7x$

Number of beads in 7 bags $= 7x$

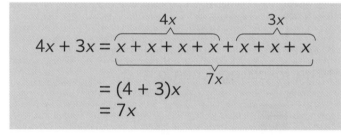

(b) How many more red beads than green beads are there?

$4x - 3x = (4 - 3)x = x$

There are more ⬜ red beads than green beads.

$$
\begin{array}{c}
\overset{4x}{\overbrace{x + x + x + x}} \\[2pt]
\underset{3x}{} \\
4x - 3x = (4 - 3)x \\
= x
\end{array}
$$

19. (a) Simplify $5r - 2r$.
$5r - 2r$
$= (5 - 2)r$
$= 3r$

There are r beads in each bag.

(b) Simplify $5r - 2r + 3r$.
$5r - 2r + 3r$
$= (5 - 2 + 3)r$
$=$ ⬚

(c) Simplify $5r - 2r + 3$.
$5r - 2r + 3$
$= (5 - 2)r + 3$
$=$ ⬚

(d) Simplify $5r + 3 - 2r + 3r$.
$5r + 3 - 2r + 3r$
$= (5 - 2 + 3)r + 3$
$=$ ⬚

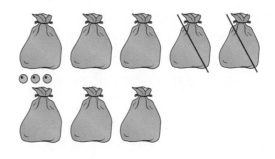

(e) Simplify $4k + 5 + 3k - 2$.
$4k + 5 + 3k - 2$
$= (4 + 3)k + (5 - 2)$
$= 7k + 3$

$4k + 3k = 7k$
$5 - 2 = 3$

20. Simplify.
   (a) $5a + 4a$
   (b) $8c - 5c$
   (c) $7k - 2k + k$
   (d) $3x + 6 - x$
   (e) $7m + 7 - 2m$
   (f) $5s + 10 + 2s$
   (g) $2y + 5 + 3y - 2$
   (h) $9 + 4m - 3m - 8$
   (i) $8r + 6 - 2r - 6$
   (j) $8p - 3p - p + 2$
   (k) $8 + 8w + 5 - 2w$
   (l) $7h + h - 4h - h$

Exercise 3, pages 144 - 145

PRACTICE A

1. Find the value of each of the following expressions when $y = 4$.
   (a) $21 - y$
   (b) $y + 25$
   (c) $3y + 2$
   (d) $3y$
   (e) $\frac{y}{2}$
   (f) $\frac{y}{16}$
   (g) $\frac{2y - 5}{4}$
   (h) $y^2 + 4$
   (i) $2y^2$
   (j) $y^3 - 20$
   (k) $\frac{3y}{2}$
   (l) $50 - 3y^2$

Simplify the following expressions.

	(a)	(b)	(c)
2.	$x + x + x$	$3x + 4x$	$6p - 4p$
3.	$2p + 2p - p$	$4r - 2r + 3r$	$5f - f - 3f$
4.	$3c - 3c + c$	$5k + 7 - k$	$6n + 3 + n + 2$
5.	$7g - 2g + 2$	$10x + 5 - 4x - 2$	$3h + 8 - 3h + 2$

6. The admission fee to a bird park is y. The admission to an amusement park is $1 more.
   (a) Express the admission fee to the amusement park in terms of y.
   (b) If the admission fee to the bird park is $8, find the admission fee to the amusement park.

7. A rope is x m long. An iron rod is 3 times as long as the rope.
   (a) Express the length of the iron rod in terms of x.
   (b) If the rope is 9 m long, how long is the iron rod?

8. Henry is x years old. Betty is 3 times as old as Henry. Peter is 4 years older than Betty.
   (a) Express Peter's age in terms of x.
   (b) If Henry is 4 years old, how old is Peter?

9. Miguel bought some bottles of milk at $2 each. He gave the cashier $50 and received $y change.
   (a) Express the number of bottles of milk Miguel bought in terms of y.
   (b) If $y = 38$, how many bottles of milk did Miguel buy?

② Integers

Negative numbers are used to represent numbers less than a starting number of 0.

Sea level is 0.
The bird is flying at an altitude of 50 m above sea level.
The submarine is 50 m below sea level. It is at a depth of −50 m.
We read **−50** as **negative fifty**.

Tom and Sam walk away from the same place but in opposite directions. Sam walks 10 m to the east. Tom walks 10 m to the west.

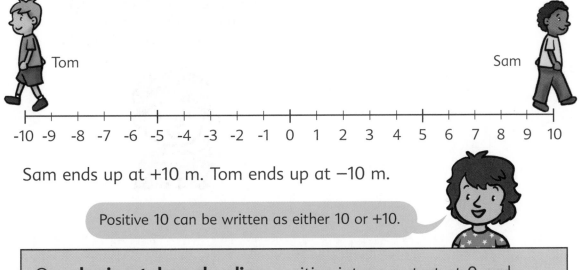

Tom   Sam

-10 -9 -8 -7 -6 -5 -4 -3 -2 -1 0 1 2 3 4 5 6 7 8 9 10

Sam ends up at +10 m. Tom ends up at −10 m.

Positive 10 can be written as either 10 or +10.

On a **horizontal number line**, positive integers start at 0 and count to the right. Negative integers start at 0 and count to the left. **0 is an integer, but it is neither negative nor positive.**

Give some other examples where both positive numbers and negative numbers are used.

1. (a) If +30 represents depositing $30 in the bank, then a withdrawal of $25 is ☐.

   (b) If +60° represents an increase in temperature of 60 degrees, then −40° represents ☐.

   (c) If +$100 means a store sold a desk at a profit of $100, then a loss of $25 is ☐.

2. What number does each letter represent?

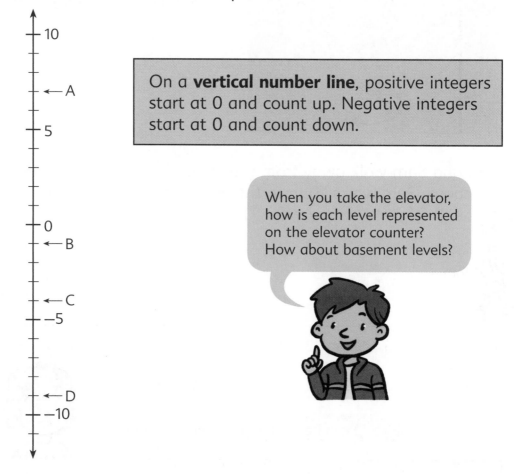

On a **vertical number line**, positive integers start at 0 and count up. Negative integers start at 0 and count down.

When you take the elevator, how is each level represented on the elevator counter? How about basement levels?

3. (a) Draw a number line to show the integers between −3 and 5.
   (b) Draw a number line to show the integers greater than −8 but less than 4.

4.

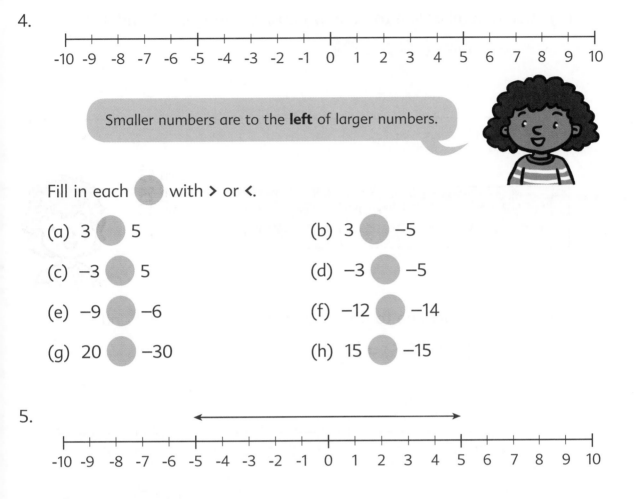

-10 -9 -8 -7 -6 -5 -4 -3 -2 -1 0 1 2 3 4 5 6 7 8 9 10

Smaller numbers are to the **left** of larger numbers.

Fill in each ⬤ with **>** or **<**.

(a) 3 ⬤ 5

(b) 3 ⬤ −5

(c) −3 ⬤ 5

(d) −3 ⬤ −5

(e) −9 ⬤ −6

(f) −12 ⬤ −14

(g) 20 ⬤ −30

(h) 15 ⬤ −15

5.

-10 -9 -8 -7 -6 -5 -4 -3 -2 -1 0 1 2 3 4 5 6 7 8 9 10

(a) The **numerical value** of −5 is 5.
What is the numerical value of 5?

On a number line, 5 and −5 are both the same distance from 0. Their numerical values are the **same**.

(b) What is the numerical value of −10?

(c) In a football game, the home team lost 20 yards in the last play. Represent this loss as a negative number, and give its numerical value.

151

Exercise 4, pages 146 - 147

6. (a) Use a number line to add two positive integers, 3 and 4.

$$(+3) + (+4) = \boxed{}$$

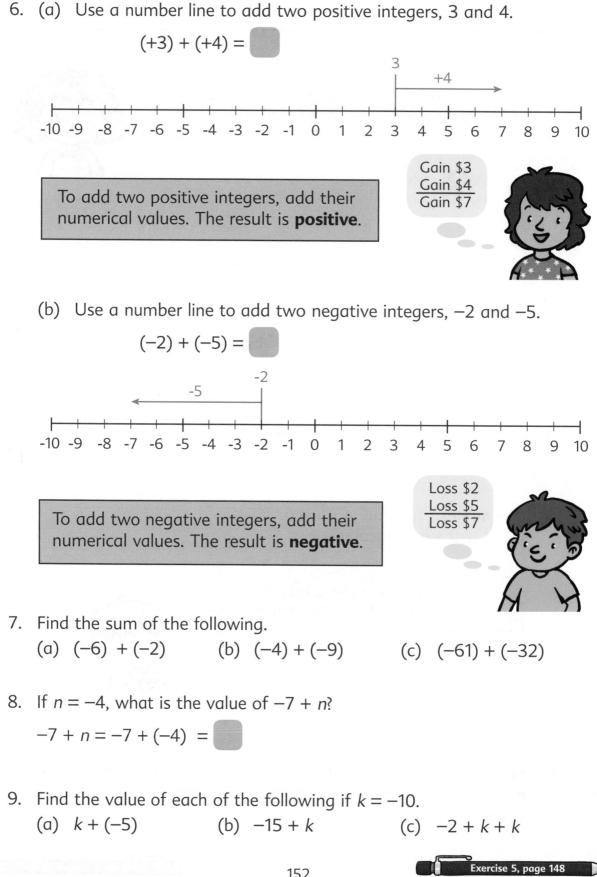

To add two positive integers, add their numerical values. The result is **positive**.

Gain $3
Gain $4
Gain $7

(b) Use a number line to add two negative integers, −2 and −5.

$$(-2) + (-5) = \boxed{}$$

To add two negative integers, add their numerical values. The result is **negative**.

Loss $2
Loss $5
Loss $7

7. Find the sum of the following.
   (a) $(-6) + (-2)$ (b) $(-4) + (-9)$ (c) $(-61) + (-32)$

8. If $n = -4$, what is the value of $-7 + n$?

   $$-7 + n = -7 + (-4) = \boxed{}$$

9. Find the value of each of the following if $k = -10$.
   (a) $k + (-5)$ (b) $-15 + k$ (c) $-2 + k + k$

152

Exercise 5, page 148

10. (a) Use a number line to find the sum of 7 and −4.

Gain \$7
Loss \$4

Gain \$3

$$(+7) + (-4) = \boxed{}$$

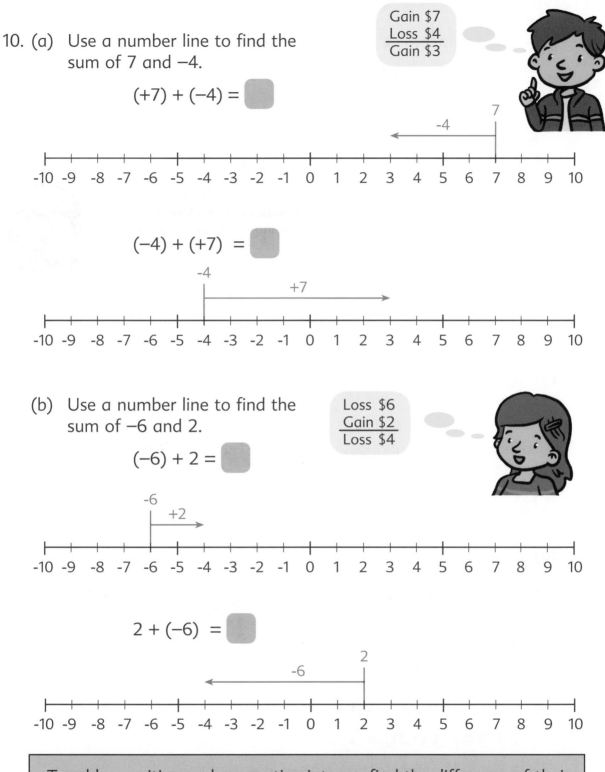

$$(-4) + (+7) = \boxed{}$$

(b) Use a number line to find the sum of −6 and 2.

Loss \$6
Gain \$2

Loss \$4

$$(-6) + 2 = \boxed{}$$

$$2 + (-6) = \boxed{}$$

To add a positive and a negative integer, find the difference of their numerical value by subtracting the smaller numerical value from the larger numerical value. If the number with the larger numerical value is positive, the result is positive. If the number with the larger numerical value is negative, the result is negative.

11. (a) Use a number line to subtract 10 from 4.

$$4 - 10 = \boxed{}$$

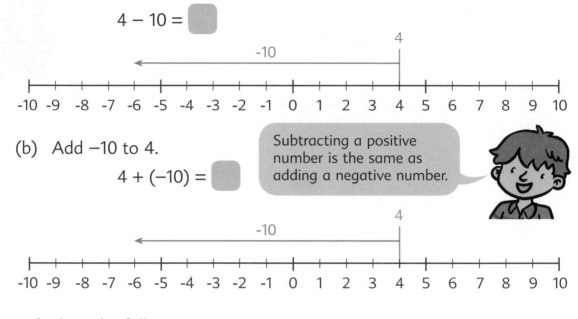

(b) Add −10 to 4.

$$4 + (-10) = \boxed{}$$

> Subtracting a positive number is the same as adding a negative number.

12. Calculate the following.
   (a) −6 + 18   (b) 23 + (−68)   (c) 30 − 42

13. A company's profits and losses for the first quarter of a year are as follows:
   January: $7000 profit
   February: $3000 loss
   March: $6000 loss

   (a) Write a mathematical expression for the company's first quarter performance.
   (b) How much loss or profit did the company make in the first quarter?

14. (a) If $n = 21$, what is the value of $7 - n$?

   $$7 - n = 7 - 21 = \boxed{}$$

   (b) If $n = -21$, what is the value of $7 + n$?

   $$7 + n = 7 + (-21) = \boxed{}$$

   (c) If $n = -21$, what is the value of $n + 7$?

   $$n + 7 = (-21) + 7 = \boxed{}$$

15. Find the value of each of the following when $p = -20$.
   (a) $p + 4$ (b) $9 + p$ (c) $p - 15$

Exercise 6, pages 149 - 150

PRACTICE B

1. (a) If 10 miles south is indicated by −10, how would you indicate 10 miles north?
   (b) If +100 indicates a profit of $100, how would a loss of $82 be indicated?
   (c) If 5 flights down is represented by −5, how would you represent 15 flights up?

2. Which is the larger number? Use the number line to find the answers.
   (a) −1, −2   (b) −6, 6   (c) −7, 2   (d) 0, −3

```
 ├──┼──┼──┼──┼──┼──┼──┼──┼──┼──┼──┼──┼──┼──┼──┼──┼──┼──┼──┼──┤
-10 -9 -8 -7 -6 -5 -4 -3 -2 -1  0  1  2  3  4  5  6  7  8  9  10
```

3. Use the number line to find find the values of the following:
   (a) $(−6) + (−1)$ (b) $−1 + 4$ (c) $−3 + 2$
   (d) $3 + (−4)$ (e) $2 + (−7)$ (f) $6 − 8$

4. Calculate the following.
   (a) $−5 + 14$ (b) $−11 + 19$ (c) $14 + (−7)$
   (d) $−9 + (−20)$ (e) $23 + (−12)$ (f) $−32 − 41$
   (g) $−36 + 22$ (h) $−45 + 18$ (i) $25 + (−66)$
   (j) $74 − 89$ (k) $101 + (−200)$ (l) $−340 + 600$
   (m) $−7 + (−11) + 9$ (n) $−10 + 16 + (−21)$ (o) $34 + (−17) + 8$
   (p) $81 − 6 − 62$ (q) $51 + 14 − 100$ (r) $−16 + 71 + 12$

5. Find the value of each of the following expressions for $n = −100$.
   (a) $−40 + n$ (b) $n − 62$ (c) $n + 320$
   (d) $n + 55$ (e) $100 + n$ (f) $22 + n$

6. An airplane descended 150 m from an altitude of 700 m and then ascended 630 m. What is the altitude of the airplane now?

③ Coordinate Graphs

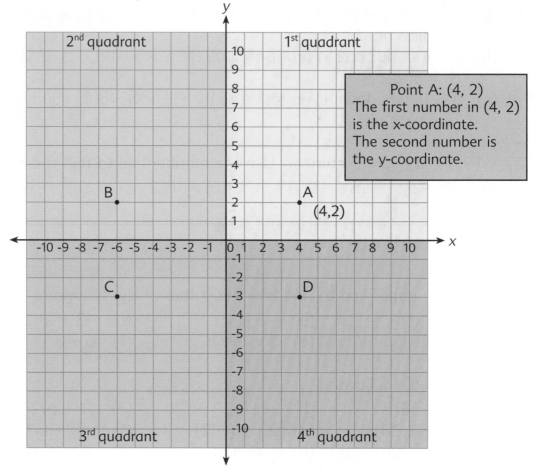

Point A: (4, 2)
The first number in (4, 2) is the x-coordinate. The second number is the y-coordinate.

A **coordinate graph** has a horizontal and a vertical number line which intersect at right angles at the point that corresponds to 0 on both number lines.

We can find any point on a graph by naming the **coordinates** of that point. These coordinates are **ordered pairs** of numbers. Remember that the first number in the pair indicates the location on the horizontal **x-axis**, and the second number indicates the location on the vertical **y-axis**.

The location of Point A in the 1st quadrant is (4, 2).
What is the location of Point B in the 2nd quadrant?
What is the location of Point C in the 3rd quadrant?
What is the location of Point D in the 4th quadrant?

The point where the two axes cross is called the **origin**. What is the ordered pair for the origin?

1.

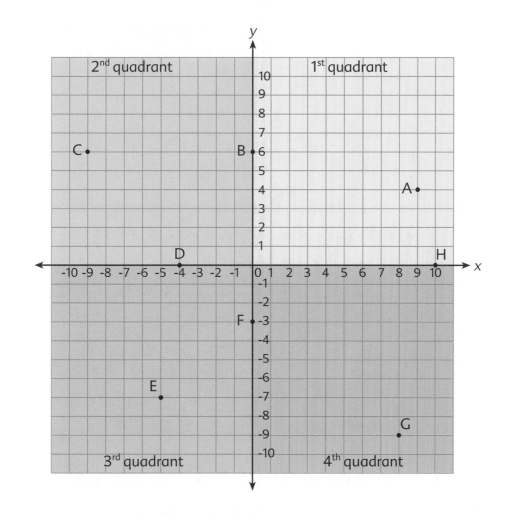

Find the coordinates of each point.

(a) A   (b) B   (c) C   (d) D

(e) E   (f) F   (g) G   (h) H

2. What are the coordinates for the intersection of the two axes?

3. In which quadrant would each of the following points be located?

(a) (6, 7)   (b) (−6, −7)   (c) (6 −7)

(d) (−6, 7)   (e) (−8, 5)   (f) (−4, −2)

Exercise 7, page 151

4.

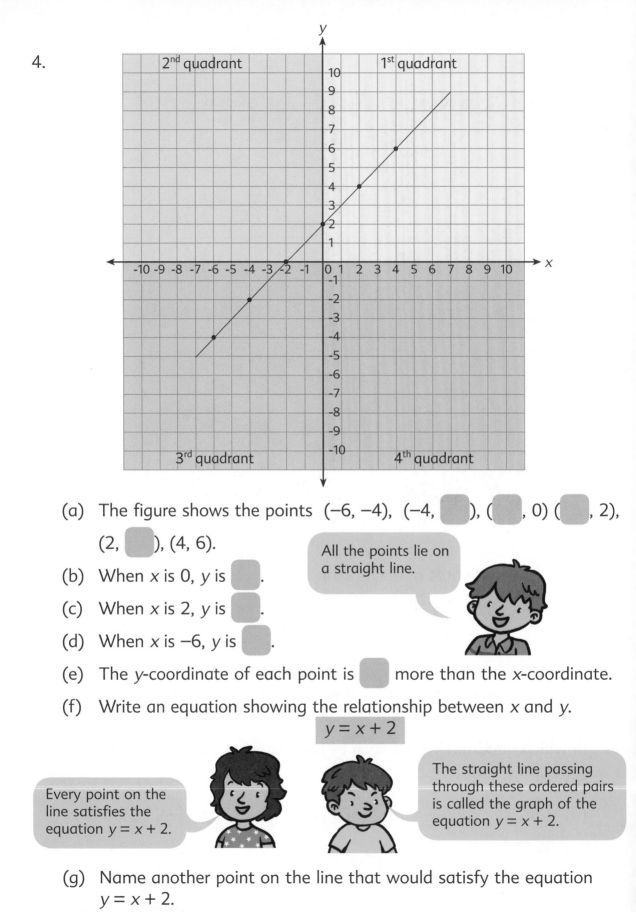

(a) The figure shows the points (−6, −4), (−4, ☐), (☐ , 0) (☐ , 2), (2, ☐), (4, 6).

> All the points lie on a straight line.

(b) When x is 0, y is ☐ .

(c) When x is 2, y is ☐ .

(d) When x is −6, y is ☐ .

(e) The y-coordinate of each point is ☐ more than the x-coordinate.

(f) Write an equation showing the relationship between x and y.

$$y = x + 2$$

> Every point on the line satisfies the equation $y = x + 2$.

> The straight line passing through these ordered pairs is called the graph of the equation $y = x + 2$.

(g) Name another point on the line that would satisfy the equation $y = x + 2$.

5. (a) Complete the table for $y = x - 3$ for values of x from -3 to 3.

x	-3	-2	-1	0	1	2	3
y	-6						
(x, y)	$(-3, -6)$						

(b) Which line is a graph of the equation $y = x - 3$?

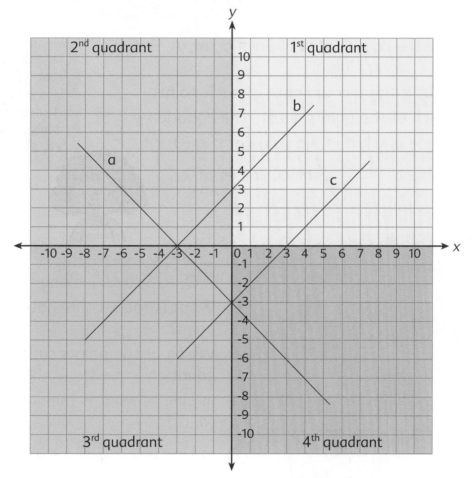

159

6.

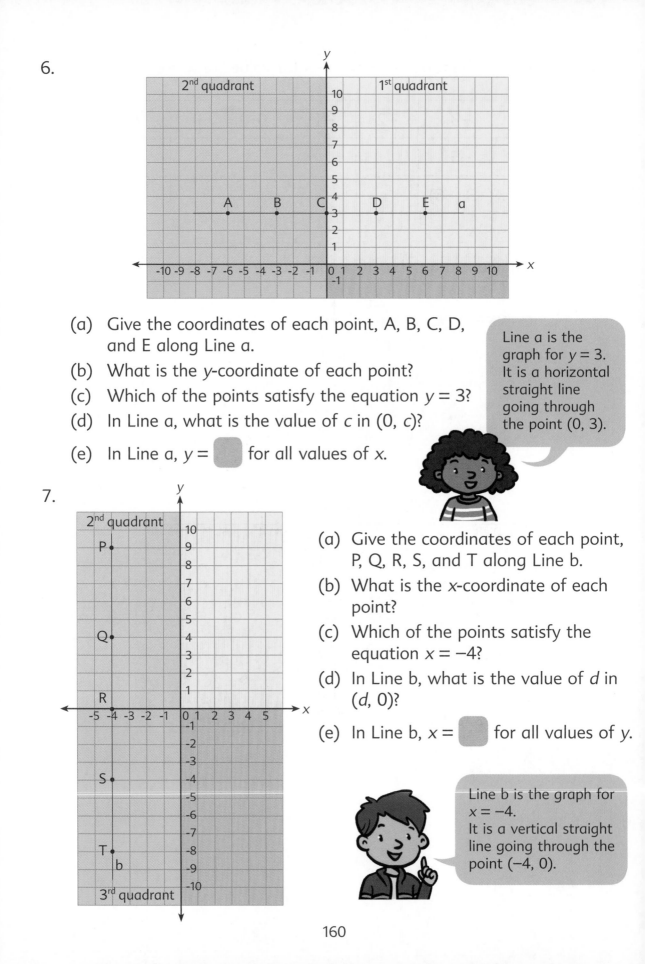

(a) Give the coordinates of each point, A, B, C, D, and E along Line a.

(b) What is the y-coordinate of each point?

(c) Which of the points satisfy the equation $y = 3$?

(d) In Line a, what is the value of c in (0, c)?

(e) In Line a, $y =$ ☐ for all values of x.

Line a is the graph for $y = 3$. It is a horizontal straight line going through the point (0, 3).

7.

(a) Give the coordinates of each point, P, Q, R, S, and T along Line b.

(b) What is the x-coordinate of each point?

(c) Which of the points satisfy the equation $x = -4$?

(d) In Line b, what is the value of d in (d, 0)?

(e) In Line b, $x =$ ☐ for all values of y.

Line b is the graph for $x = -4$. It is a vertical straight line going through the point (−4, 0).

8.

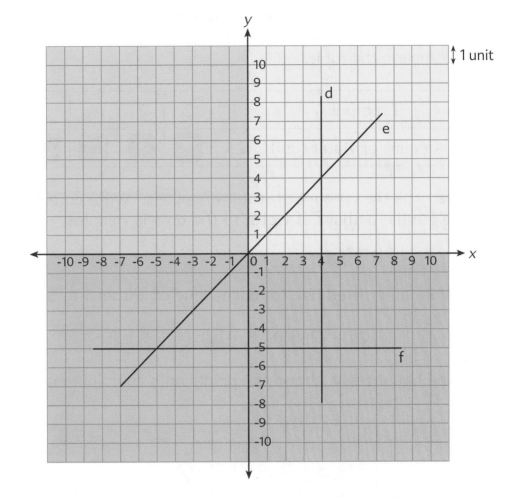

(a) Give the coordinates for the intersection of Lines d and e.

(b) Give the cooordinates for the intersection of Lines d and f.

(c) Give the cooordinates for the intersection of Lines e and f.

(d) Any point on Line ▢ has an x-coordinate of 4.

(e) Which coordinate is −5 for any point on Line f?

(f) Write an equation for the Line e.

$$y = ▢$$

161

Exercise 8, page 152

9. Water is flowing from a tap at the rate of 25 gal per minute.

(a) Complete the table.

Time (min)	1	2	3	4	5	x
Amount of water (gal)	25					

(b) Let y be the amount of water in gallons. Write an equation to relate the amount of water to the time in minutes.

$$y = \boxed{} x$$

(c) Write an ordered pair for each value of x from 1 to 5.

(1, 25), (2, 50), (3, ⬛), (4, ⬛), (5, ⬛)

(d) The figure below shows the points on a coordinate graph.

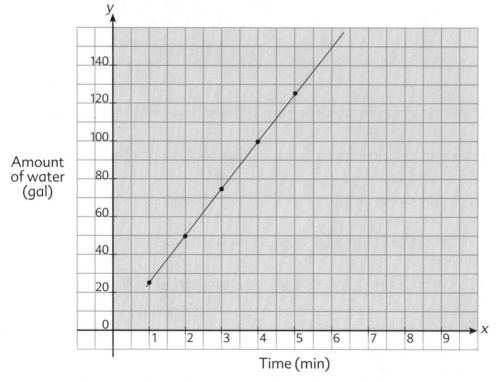

Time (min)

Does the graph of the equation go through the origin?

(e) Use the graph to find how long it takes for 150 gallons to flow from the tap.

10. (a) Complete the table for the equation $y = 2x + (-3)$ for values of x from 0 to 5.

x	0	1	2	3	4	5
y						
(x, y)						

(b) Which line is the graph for $y = 2x + (-3)$?

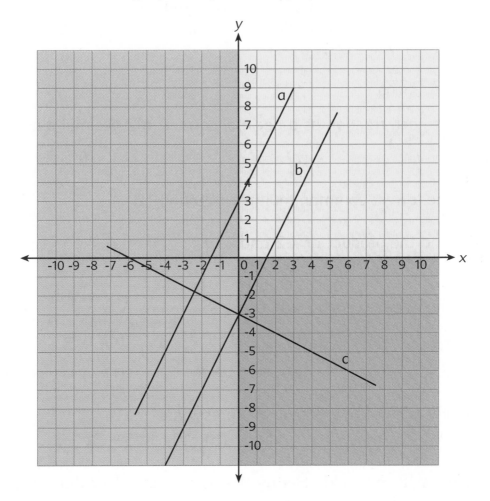

(c) Use the graph to find the value of y for x-coordinate = −3.

(d) What is the value of x for y-coordinate = −5?

163

Exercise 9, pages 153 - 154

REVIEW 13

1. What is the missing number in each ▢?

   (a) The digit 3 in 40,837,405 stands for 3 × ▢.

   (b) The value of the digit 6 in 2.067 is ▢.

2. In 6,543,000, what is the digit in the ten thousands place?

3. Write each of the following as a decimal.
   (a) 3 hundredths + 8 tenths + 6 hundreds
   (b) 8 and four hundredths
   (c) 0.03 + 7 + 0.001
   (d) $45 + \dfrac{9}{1000}$

4. Express each fraction as a decimal correct to 2 decimal places.

   (a) $\dfrac{4}{7}$ (b) $\dfrac{5}{6}$ (c) $3\dfrac{2}{9}$

5. Find the lowest common multiple of 8 and 12.

6. (a) Find the product of 4.2 and 1.19.
   (b) Find the quotient of 4.59 divided by 0.6.

7. Find the value of each y when $x = 15$.

   (a) $y = \dfrac{8x}{3}$ (b) $y = 3x + 7$ (c) $y = 2x^2$

   (d) $y = 22 - x$ (e) $y = \dfrac{x}{2} - x$ (f) $y = (-x) + 28$

8. Simplify each of the following expressions.
   (a) $14y - 5y + 7$ (b) $10y + 15 - 3y - 8$

9. Keisha is 12 years old. Her mother is m years older than she.
   (a) How old will her mother be in 5 years' time? Give the answer in terms of m.
   (b) If $m = 20$, how old will her mother be in 5 years' time?

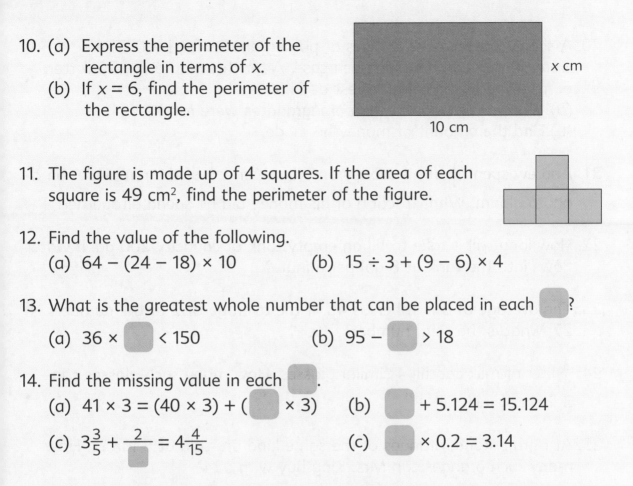

10. (a) Express the perimeter of the
        rectangle in terms of x.
    (b) If $x = 6$, find the perimeter of
        the rectangle.

x cm

10 cm

11. The figure is made up of 4 squares. If the area of each
    square is 49 cm², find the perimeter of the figure.

12. Find the value of the following.
    (a) $64 - (24 - 18) \times 10$ (b) $15 \div 3 + (9 - 6) \times 4$

13. What is the greatest whole number that can be placed in each ⬜?

    (a) $36 \times$ ⬜ < 150 (b) $95 -$ ⬜ > 18

14. Find the missing value in each ⬜.
    (a) $41 \times 3 = (40 \times 3) + ($ ⬜ $\times 3)$ (b) ⬜ $+ 5.124 = 15.124$

    (c) $3\frac{3}{5} + \dfrac{2}{⬜} = 4\frac{4}{15}$ (c) ⬜ $\times 0.2 = 3.14$

15. A copy machine can print at the rate of 90 similar copies every
    5 minutes. How long will it take to print 270 such copies?

16. A machine caps 160 similar bottles every 2 minutes. At this rate, how
    long does it take to cap 400 bottles of the same kind?

17. A rectangular field is 90 m long and 60 m wide. What is the ratio of the
    length to the width of the field? Give the answer in its simplest form.

18. 15 similar shirts cost $35. If 2 of them are sold at $4.90 each, and
    the rest are sold at $2.50 each, find the amount of money made.

19. Mary has 200 coins. 98 of them are commemorative coins. What
    percentage of the coins are commemorative coins?

20. A shopkeeper bought 8 cases of pomegranates for $400. There were 50 pomegranates in each case. After throwing away 20 rotten pomegranates, he sold the rest at $1.50 each.
    (a) What percentage of the pomegranates were rotten?
    (b) Find the amount of money he made.

21. Andrew spent $\frac{1}{4}$ of his money on a book and $\frac{1}{2}$ of the remainder on a photo album. What fraction of his money did he spend altogether?

22. How long will it take to fill an empty tank of capacity 200 gal if water flows into the tank at 8 gal per minute?

23. The average of 3 numbers is 45. If the average of 2 of the numbers is 27, what is the third number?

24. $\frac{3}{4}$ liter of milk can fill 4 similar glasses. How many such glasses can 3 liters of milk fill?

25. At a fruit stand, oranges of the same kind are sold at 5 for $2. How many such oranges can Mrs. King buy with $24?

26. In each of the following figures, not drawn to scale, find $\angle x$.
    (a) ABC is a straight line.   (b)

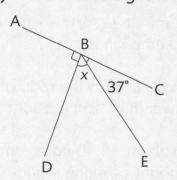

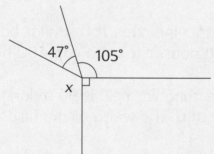

27. The pie chart shows how a group of students travel to school. What percentage of the students walk to school?

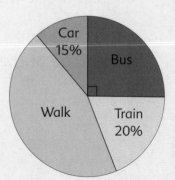

28. The pie chart represents the number of people on a cruise. $\frac{1}{8}$ of the people were girls.

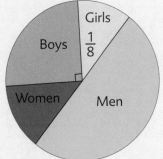

(a) What fraction of the people were boys?
(b) What fraction of the people were women?
(c) There were 120 girls on the cruise. How many people were there altogether?

29. The line graph shows the sales of T-shirts over 5 months.

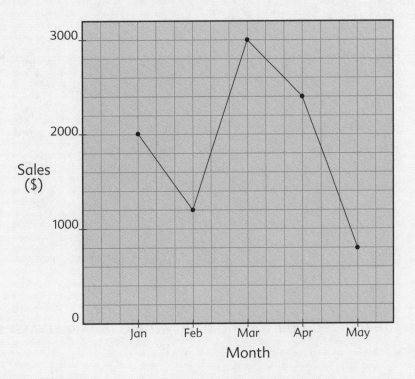

(a) What was the increase in sales from February to March?
(b) What was the average monthly sales?
(c) If each T-shirt was sold for $4 in April, how many T-shirts were sold that month?

30. In which quadrant of the coordinate graph would each of the following points be located?

(a) (6, 7)   (b) (−6, −7)   (c) (6, −7)

(d) (−6, 7)   (e) (−8, 5)   (f) (−4, −2)

31.

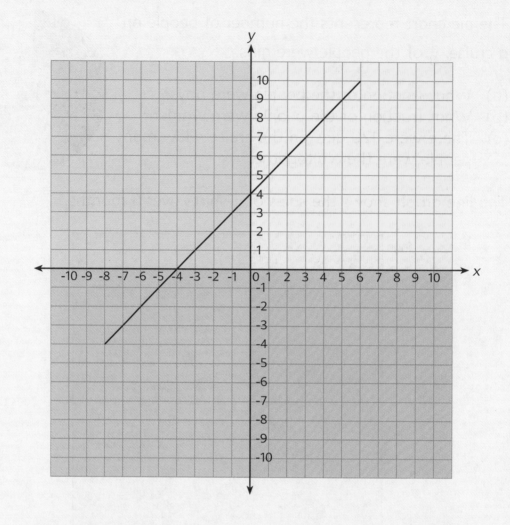

(a) Write the ordered pair for the point where the line crosses the x-axis.

(b) The point (1, ⬜) is on the line.

(c) Create a table comparing the values of x and y. Then write an equation for the line.

32. The histogram shows the number of points 5th graders scored on a science test.

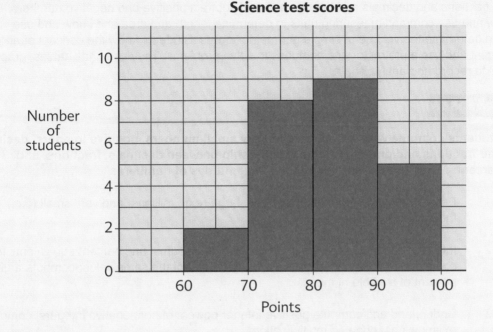

Science test scores

Number of students (y-axis): 0, 2, 4, 6, 8, 10

Points (x-axis): 60, 70, 80, 90, 100

(a) Find the number of students whose scores are represented on the histogram.

(b) How many points are represented in each interval?

(c) How many students scored at least 90 points but fewer than 100 points?

(d) In what interval did the greatest number of students score?

(e) In what interval did the fewest number of students score?

(f) What percentage of the students scored at least 70 points but fewer than 80 points?

(g) What fraction of the students scored at least 80 points but fewer than 90 points?

Review 13, pages 155 - 160

Grade Five Mathematics Content Standards

By the end of grade five, students increase their facility with the four basic arithmetic operations applied to fractions and decimals and learn to add and subtract positive and negative numbers. They know and use common measuring units to determine length and area and know and use formulas to determine the volume of simple geometric figures. Students know the concept of angle measurement and use a protractor and compass to solve problems. They use grids, tables, graphs, and charts to record and analyze data.

Number Sense

1.0 Students compute with very large and very small numbers, positive integers, decimals, and fractions and understand the relationship between decimals, fractions, and percents. They understand the relative magnitudes of numbers:

1.1 Estimate, round, and manipulate very large (e.g., millions) and very small (e.g., thousandths) numbers.

1.2 Interpret percents as a part of a hundred; find decimal and percent equivalents for common fractions and explain why they represent the same value; compute a given percent of a whole number.

1.3 Understand and compute positive integer powers of nonnegative integers; compute examples as repeated multiplication.

1.4 Determine the prime factors of all numbers through 50 and write the numbers as the product of their prime factors by using exponents to show multiples of a factor (e.g., $24 = 2 \times 2 \times 2 \times 3 = 2^3 \times 3$).

1.5 Identify and represent on a number line decimals, fractions, mixed numbers, and positive and negative integers.

2.0 Students perform calculations and solve problems involving addition, subtraction, and simple multiplication and division of fractions and decimals:

2.1 Add, subtract, multiply, and divide with decimals; add with negative integers; subtract positive integers from negative integers; and verify the reasonableness of the results.

2.2 Demonstrate proficiency with division, including division with positive decimals and long division with multi-digit divisors.

2.3 Solve simple problems, including ones arising in concrete situations, involving the addition and subtraction of fractions and mixed numbers (like and unlike denominators of 20 or less), and express answers in the simplest form.

2.4 Understand the concept of multiplication and division of fractions.

2.5 Compute and perform simple multiplication and division of fractions and apply these procedures to solving problems.

Algebra and Functions

1.0   Students use variables in simple expressions, compute the value of the expression for specific values of the variable, and plot and interpret the results:

1.1   Use information taken from a graph or equation to answer questions about a problem situation.

1.2   Use a letter to represent an unknown number; write and evaluate simple algebraic expressions in one variable by substitution.

1.3   Know and use the distributive property in equations and expressions with variables.

1.4   Identify and graph ordered pairs in the four quadrants of the coordinate plane.

1.5   Solve problems involving linear functions with integer values; write the equation; and graph the resulting ordered pairs of integers on a grid.

Measurement and Geometry

1.0   Students understand and compute the volumes and areas of simple objects:

1.1   Derive and use the formula for the area of a triangle and of a parallelogram by comparing each with the formula for the area of a rectangle (i.e., two of the same triangles make a parallelogram with twice the area; a parallelogram is compared with a rectangle of the same area by pasting and cutting a right triangle on the parallelogram).

1.2   Construct a cube and rectangular box from two-dimensional patterns and use these patterns to compute the surface area for these objects.

1.3   Understand the concept of volume and use the appropriate units in common measuring systems (i.e., cubic centimeter [cm^3], cubic meter [m^3], cubic inch [$in.^3$], cubic yard [$yd.^3$]) to compute the volume of rectangular solids.

1.4   Differentiate between, and use appropriate units of measures for, two- and three-dimensional objects (i.e., find the perimeter, area, volume).

2.0   Students identify, describe, and classify the properties of, and the relationships between, plane and solid geometric figures:

2.1   Measure, identify, and draw angles, perpendicular and parallel lines, rectangles, and triangles by using appropriate tools (e.g., straightedge, ruler, compass, protractor, drawing software).

2.2   Know that the sum of the angles of any triangle is 180° and the sum of the angles of any quadrilateral is 360° and use this information to solve problems.

2.3   Visualize and draw two-dimensional views of three-dimensional objects made from rectangular solids.

Statistics, Data Analysis, and Probability

1.0   Students display, analyze, compare, and interpret different data sets, including data sets of different sizes:

    1.1   Know the concepts of mean, median, and mode; compute and compare simple examples to show that they may differ.

    1.2   Organize and display single-variable data in appropriate graphs and representations (e.g., histogram, circle graphs) and explain which types of graphs are appropriate for various data sets.

    1.3   Use fractions and percentages to compare data sets of different sizes.

    1.4   Identify ordered pairs of data from a graph and interpret the meaning of the data in terms of the situation depicted by the graph.

    1.5   Know how to write ordered pairs correctly; for example, (x, y).

Mathematical Reasoning

1.0   Students make decisions about how to approach problems:

    1.1   Analyze problems by identifying relationships, distinguishing relevant from irrelevant information, sequencing and prioritizing information, and observing patterns.

    1.2   Determine when and how to break a problem into simpler parts.

2.0   Students use strategies, skills, and concepts in finding solutions:

    2.1   Use estimation to verify the reasonableness of calculated results.

    2.2   Apply strategies and results from simpler problems to more complex problems.

    2.3   Use a variety of methods, such as words, numbers, symbols, charts, graphs, tables, diagrams, and models, to explain mathematical reasoning.

    2.4   Express the solution clearly and logically by using the appropriate mathematical notation and terms and clear language; support solutions with evidence in both verbal and symbolic work.

    2.5   Indicate the relative advantages of exact and approximate solutions to problems and give answers to a specified degree of accuracy.

    2.6   Make precise calculations and check the validity of the results from the context of the problem.

3.0   Students move beyond a particular problem by generalizing to other situations:

   3.1   Evaluate the reasonableness of the solution in the context of the original situation.

   3.2   Note the method of deriving the solution and demonstrate a conceptual understanding of the derivation by solving similar problems.

   3.3   Develop generalizations of the results obtained and apply them in other circumstances.

GLOSSARY

Word	Meaning
average	The total value of a set of data, divided by the number or frequency of that data.
coordinates	We can find any point on a graph by naming the **coordinates** of that point. These are ordered pairs of numbers. Example: Point A: (4, 2). The first number, 4, in (4, 2) is the x-coordinate. The second number, 2, is the y-coordinate.
graph	A (coordinate) graph has a horizontal and a vertical number line, called x-axis and y-axis respectively. The two lines intersect at the point (0, 0), called the origin.

Word	Meaning
histogram	A **histogram** is a chart or bar graph that makes it easy to see data grouped in intervals. **Mathematics test scores** Number of students (y-axis: 0, 2, 4, 6, 8, 10) Points (x-axis: 60, 70, 80, 90, 100) Bars: 60–70 = 2, 70–80 = 8, 80–90 = 10, 90–100 = 4
mean, median and mode	**Mean** is the average of a list of data. **Median** is the midpoint in a series of numbers; the middle or 'halfway' value. **Mode** is the most frequently occurring value in the data set; the value that appears the most often.
rate	1. A quantity measured with respect to another measured quantity; e.g. a rate of speed of 60 miles an hour. 2. A measure of a part with respect to a whole; a proportion; e.g. the mortality rate; a tax rate. 3. The cost per unit of a commodity or service; e.g. postal rates.

Index